# K.I.S.S.
## FOOTBALL

# K.I.S.S.
# FOOTBALL

## Keep it Simple and Sound

## ROBERT GAVETTE

ARPress
ILLUMINATING IDEAS
EMPOWERING VOICES

**ARPress**
45 Dan Road Suite 36
Canton MA 02021

Hotline: 1(800) 220-7660
Fax:     1(855) 752-6001

Ordering Information:
Quantity sales. Special discounts are available on quantity purchases by corporations, associations, and others. For details, contact the publisher at the address above.

Printed in the United States of America.

ISBN-13:   Paperback      979-8-89389-866-8
           Hardcover      979-8-89389-867-5
           eBook          979-8-89389-868-2

Library of Congress Control Number:   2024923860

Special thanks to Adrian Barragan for all the help
he gave in the construction of this book.

# CONTENTS

# DEDICATION

This book is dedicated to administrators, parents, associates, and friends who, in many ways, contributed to our success in football; also to the athletes who showed up every day to football practice and endured long practice hours of being tired, sweaty, hurt, bruised, literally exhausted, but kept the spirit of the game alive and well.

I will always cherish the fact that the athletes entrusted on us their physical, mental, and complete dedication with no conditions or limitations. Coaching young adolescents and young adults was a priceless experience. After thirty-seven years of coaching in six different schools with twenty-seven championship credits to our name, we learned that "the dedication of our athletes is what makes our successes possible." We placed very high performance expectations on our athletes, and they never wavered; they gave more. Our motto over the dressing room door still stands: "Winners never quit, and quitters never win."

# OFFENSIVE PHILOSOPHY

In organizing an "offensive package," one must consider any and all options available to a coach and how to implement this package and does it provide a "simple" as well as a "sound" approach with a baseline that allows the coach and his team to achieve a reasonable chance to build a respected football program.

One must avoid a tendency to implement a conglomeration of runs and passes instead of perfecting the execution of "simple and sound" plays that fit the skills and experience of the team concept. "If you fail to plan, then you plan to fail."

# INTRODUCTION

This book contains proven approaches, ideas, and schemes that come from attending many coaching clinics and from years of coaching experience. My intentions are to help you prepare your team in a positive and simplistic manner. In my book, you will complete a tried and proven system to attack and control the defense. These basic tools will help you prepare your players for success, regardless of your level of experience as a coach or that of your athletes as less experienced players. Numbers, letters, and code-words are used throughout the book in order to facilitate communication between players and their coaches. Always keep in mind that "if you fail to prepare, you prepare to fail."

# BOOK INTRODUCTION

To any coach, at any level, this book is intended to help you get started in coaching. It will offer several "proven" approaches, ideas and schemes that I have acquired through years of experience and knowledge from the many coaching clinics that I have attended and the books I have read.

I experimented with several systems and soon discovered that the basic approach is somewhat similar. I have set out to simplify the many approaches into the system of numbers and code words to further simplify the process of teaching football. The run, the pass, the back numbers, and the hole numbers are the same as in other systems, but I went with the purpose of further simplifying the whole game into a package that can be utilized by anyone at any level of experience.

In this book, you will find a complete, tried, and proven system to attack and control the defense at every angle with all the basic tools at your fingertips regardless of the *level of experience of the coach or of the players.*

The era of three-yards and cloud-of-dust football is a thing of the past. We know this, yet many are still reluctant to change the old-school approach. There are many approaches that are being used by the many innovative offensive and defensive coaches that

if you are not prepared to neutralize the defense with more than one bullet in the chamber, the ride on the bus back from the game is going to be a long one.

The intent of this book is to present in a simple fashion a coach with enough information to implement a complete program. The number system will allow you to communicate with three numbers any running play or any pass play. The line sets have simple, descriptive "code words." The passing tree has the same numbers for all potential receivers. There are also numbers for the backs, numbers for the backfield sets, numbers for the LOS (line-of-scrimmage), and numbers for defensive techniques.

One of the reasons numbers are used throughout the book is they help facilitate communication. Most, if not all, of the "code words" are common football terms (e.g., *Pro Rt. 108 Sweep* or *Slot Rt.-Sprint Rt. 664 Pass*). I also use acronyms, such as LOS, FG (field goal), PAT (point-after-touchdown), POA (point-of-attack), which are self-explanatory as using the complete phrase.

A final note, use this book completely or parts of it as the rest will be left up to the coach's discretion. Even though winning can never be a guaranteed result, it is critical that no page is left unturned for the coach and his players to leave the practice field confident. "He who fails to prepare prepares to fail." Good luck and many "happy bus rides home."

A coach's d/ream is to have all his athletes who show up on the first days of practice 100 percent ready mentally and physically. To achieve this, the athletes must be willing to be polished and to listen, learn, and perform; ready to win every game and make the coach famous and recognized as an automatic winner.

Let the truth be known that, in sports, nothing is easy or automatic. Rather, it is slow, tedious, repetitious, and time-consuming.

Winning is never guaranteed unless there is an ingredient of a genuine and sincere effort to improve and a strong will to never accept losing as an alternative. This should remind us of a famous saying that goes, "Those who stay will be champions."

Now that we are ready to get off the "soapbox," let us sit back and observe each player as an individual. As you walk up to him and initially observe his many "mistakes," ask yourself what you did beforehand to introduce him to the technique, method, or maneuver that will enlighten him to understand your demands on him. Make sure to spark his initiative with information, and most importantly, show some patience. Before you know it, he will surprise you above and beyond your expectations with a "smile" and say, "Thanks, Coach. Now what else do you want me to learn today?"

# THE GAME OF FOOTBALL

A GAME THAT IS NOT FOR ALL,
IT IS NOT FOR THE SMALL,
NOT EVEN FOR THE TALL.

IT IS A GAME FOR A MAN,
IT IS PLAYED ALL OVER THE LAND,
SOMETIMES EVEN IN THE SAND.

A GAME WHERE YOU NEED TO BE TOUGH,
BECAUSE SOMETIMES IT GETS MIGHTY ROUGH.

IF YOU DARE, YOU MUST PREPARE
BECAUSE IT WILL GIVE YOU A SCARE.

IT WILL BRING PRAISE, IT WILL BRING SCORN,
BUT WE'LL PLAY IT EVEN IN A STORM.

IT IS A GAME FOR ALL SEASONS BUT NOT
FOR ALL REASONS, FOR IT IS ROUGH AND
SURELY FOR THOSE WHO ARE TOUGH.

WE WILL PLAY IT FOR A WHILE AND LEAVE IT
AND ONLY SMILE WHEN WE REMEMBER THAT
ONLY IN SEPTEMBER AND IN NOVEMBER IT STARTS
AND IT ENDS FOR ME AND MY FRIENDS.

WHO WAS THE TOUGHEST? WHO WAS THE
ROUGHEST? WHO WILL REMEMBER AFTER DECEMBER?

I WILL REMEMBER AND NEVER BE SORRY THAT
I HAD A CHANCE TO TELL THE STORY . . .

Unknown Author

# K.I.S.S. FOOTBALL

*Keeping It Simple and Sound*

A suggested process will begin with these steps:

1.  The huddle
2.  Quarterback and halfback dual roles
3.  A complete offensive package
4.  The offensive line - hole numbers
5.  The backfield - numbers and set
6.  Backfield sets - 100, 200, 300, 400
7.  Quarterbacks - steps, angles, reads
8.  Backs - FB, HB - aim points, mesh points
9.  Veer - inside, outside - read, options
10. Veer - line spacing and calls, rules
11. Line blocking schemes (by the numbers):
    #No. 1  Dives - base or rule block
    #No. 2  Blast or lead – double-team block
    #No. 3  Belly - cross block
    #No. 4  Trap - across the ball, "G" away from ball
    #No. 5  Veer - read #No. 2, #No. 4 holes, release last man LOS
    #No. 0  Sweep - reach block

12. Passing game basics

    A.  Play action pass - aggressive blocks playside
    B.  Sprint pass - aggie play side, cup backside
    C.  Drop back pass - cup block, turn out block

13. Motion back offense= (Run – Pass – Trap – Decoy)

# BASIC SETS – PRO – SLOT – WING

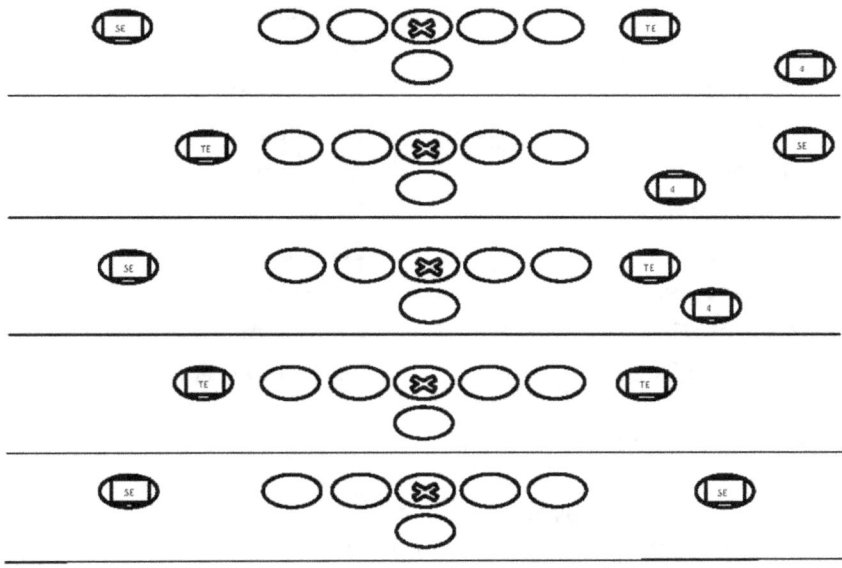

Commonly used football terms:

| | |
|---|---|
| 1. LOS | 15. Twins |
| 2. Corner | 16. Trips |
| 3. Flag | 17. Slot |
| 4. Post | 18. Wing |
| 5. Chain | 19. Delay |
| 6. Hash marks | 20. Seal Block |
| 7. Sideline | 21. Combo |
| 8. Drag | 22. Lead |
| 9. Shotgun | 23. Load |
| 10. Motion | 24. Wheel |
| 11. Flex | 25. Victory |
| 12. Reverse | 26. Blitz |
| 13. Split End | 27. Scramble |
| 14. Wide Receiver | 28. Pump Fake |

Introducing an offensive system:

1. Classroom - playbook
2. Line of scrimmage - hole numbering system
3. Backs - numbers by position
4. Backfield sets - 100, 200, 300, 400
5. The huddle
6. Quarterback calls: The run

   A. Formation (code word)
   B. Blocking scheme
   C. Hole number
   D. Snap count

Communication – Progression – Execution

# RULE BLOCKING = BY NUMBER/CODE WORD

"1"  Dive - base (rule) blocking - in, on, off, outside

"2"  Blast/Lead - double-team block at the hole (POA) FB blast blocked on LB (soft spot of defense)

"3"  Belly - cross block at the hole (POA) the outside lineman goes first

"4"  Trap/Counter - guard traps across the ball, the fullback seals blocks for pulling guard

"5"  Veer - veer read by QB at hole #No. 2 or #No. 3 inside veer, outside veer read by QB at hole #No. 4 or #No. 5

"0"  Sweep - reach block by any uncovered lineman Jet sweep is an "all-go situation."


"SPECIALS"

Code Words Added to Play

"G" or George = guard kick block on defensive end

"I" or Tiger = tackle trap across the ball

"Box" or "Slot" = #No. 4 back on split end side (tight/flexed)

"Wing" or "Pro" = #No. 4 back on tight end side (tight/flexed)

"W-Trap" = #No. 4 back in motion goes to POA and traps

# INSIDE VEER BLOCKING
# (124 VEER-WEAK SIDE)

| | |
|---|---|
| 1-1 | Center = Base block 1. Gap to 2. Man on 3. Nearest linebacker. |
| #No. 1 | On Guard = Base block 1. Gap away 2. Man on 3. Nearest linebacker. |
| 1-2 | On Tackle = Base block 1. Down to inside 2. Combo with guard to LB. |
| #No. 1 | On Tight End = 3 step release outside block middle 1/3 (pitch support). |
| #No. 1 | On Split End = Stalk block deep outside 1/3. |
| #No. 2 | On Flanker = Stalk block pitch support. |
| **Note:** | Quarterback = 2 step 45°, behind on-side guard, read dive-key (DT) 30° at keep-in-pitch-key (DE) |
| | Fullback = Attack the outside heel of the guard Pitch back = Keep pitch angle with quarterback |

# OUTSIDE VEER BLOCKING (125 VEER-STRONG SIDE)

| | |
|---|---|
| 1-2 | Center = Zone or base block backside. |
| #No. 1 | On Guard = Base block 1. Gap away 2. Man on 3. Nearest linebacker. |
| #No. 2 | On Tackle = Base block 1. Gap away 2. Man on 3. Nearest linebacker. |
| 2-1 | On Tight End = Base block down to your inside double team with tackle or combo to linebacker. |
| **Note:** | Quarterback = Drive off opposite foot to a point directly behind your offensive tackle, read keep-pitch-key Fullback = Attack the outside heel of the guard |
| | Pitch back = Keep pitch angle with quarterback |

# ORGANIZATION: OFFENSIVE SYSTEM

I. BACKFIELD SETS: (WITH MOTION BACK)

100
200      OR SHOTGUN
300      QB UNDER CENTER
400

II. LINE SETS: BALANCED, UNBALANCED

PRO
WING     RIGHT OR LEFT
SLOT

SPREAD - 2 WIDE RECEIVERS
"2" TIGHT ENDS

III. LINE BLOCKING SCHEMES: THE RUN

#No. 1. BASE                 #No. 4. TRAP/COUNTER
#No. 2. SLANT                #No. 5. VEER (FLEX)
#No. 3. BELLY                #No. 0. SWEEPS

IV. LINE BLOCKING SCHEMES: THE PASS

A.  DROP BACK PASS - CUP BLOCK (TURN OUT BLOCK)
B.  SPRINTOUTS - AGGIE PLAYSIDE
C.  PLAY ACTION - AGGIE PLAYSIDE
D.  SCREENS - LEFT, RIGHT, AND MIDDLE
E.  #No. 4 HB PASS

## V. BASIC PASS ATTACK

1. DROP BACK - 3-5-7 STEPS
2. SPRINT PASS - RIGHT OR LEFT
3. HB-FB DRAW - (QB DRAW)
4. SCREENS LEFT, MIDDLE, RIGHT
5. BOOTLEG RIGHT OR LEFT PASS
6. SWEEP PASS - QB THROWBACK
7. PLAY ACTION PASS (3 STEP) (SELL THE RUN)
8. HB OR TE DELAY (SHORT SCREEN)
9. HOT RECEIVER (TE OR WR) VERSUS BLITZ
10. OUTLET RECEIVER (CHIP BLOCK)
11. #No. 4 BACK "MOTION BACK" OBJECTIVES

    A. RECEIVER, BLOCKER, PASSER, DECOY
    B. FORCE DEFENSIVE ADJUSTMENTS
    C. STRETCH DEFENSE VERTICALLY/HORIZONTALLY
    D. FORCE LINEBACKER COVERAGE
    E. OVERLOAD DEFENSIVE AREAS

12. OPTION ROUTES:

    A. DRAG          E. SOFT SPOT
    B. STOP          F. BACK SHOULDER
    C. CHAIN         G. SEAM
    D. COMEBACK

Backfield Numbering and Sets

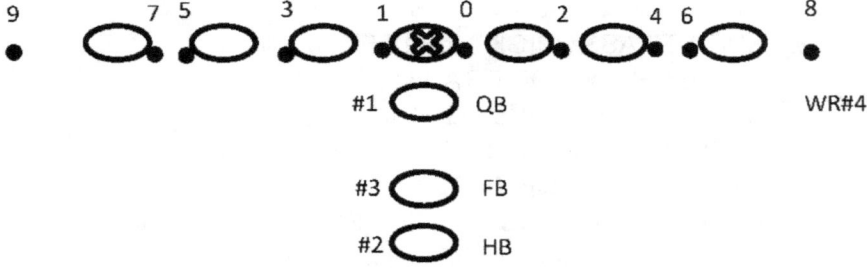

4 Backfield Sets: 100, 200, 300, 400

NOTE: The #No. 4 back is the motion back, even though any back can be put in motion from any backfield set.

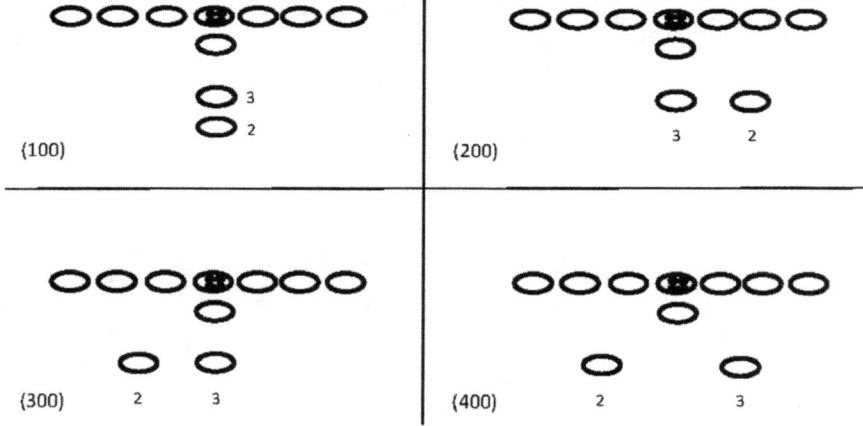

Coaches's Notes:

# Basic Formations: To Start an Offense

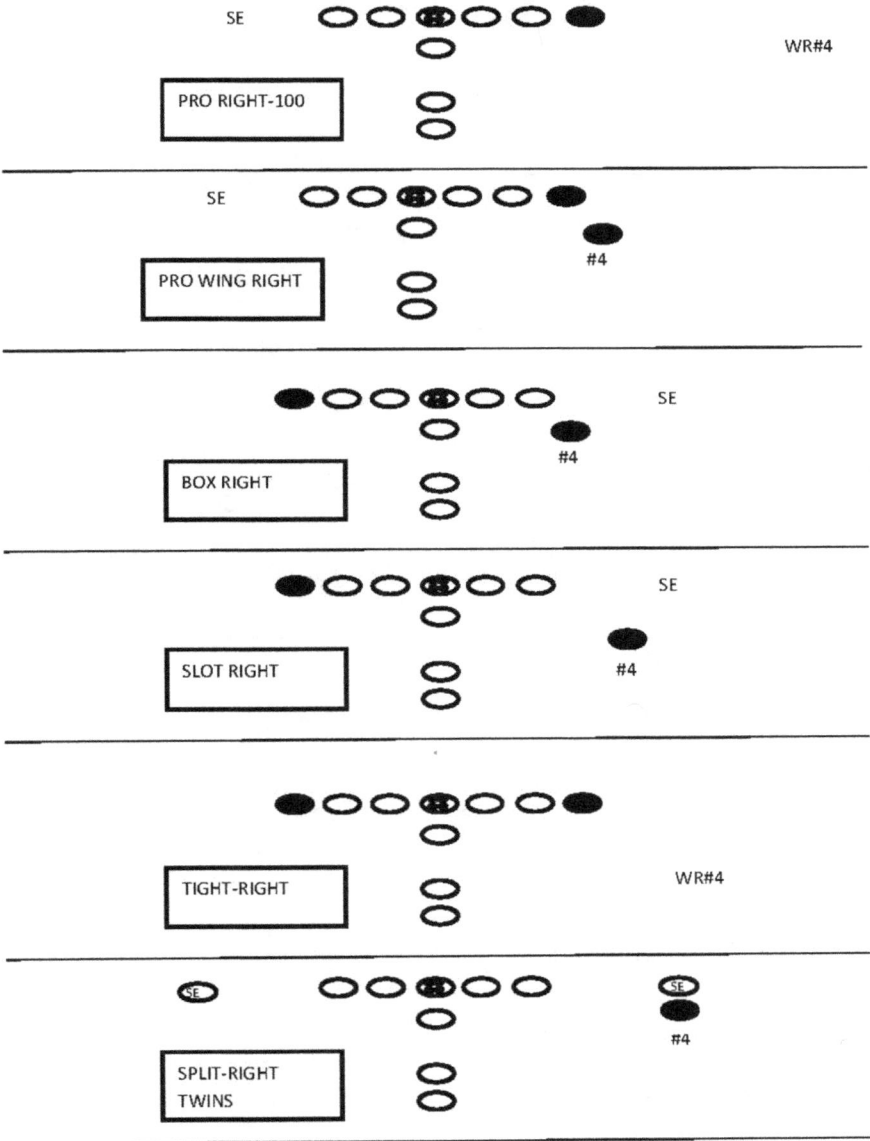

Coach's Notes:

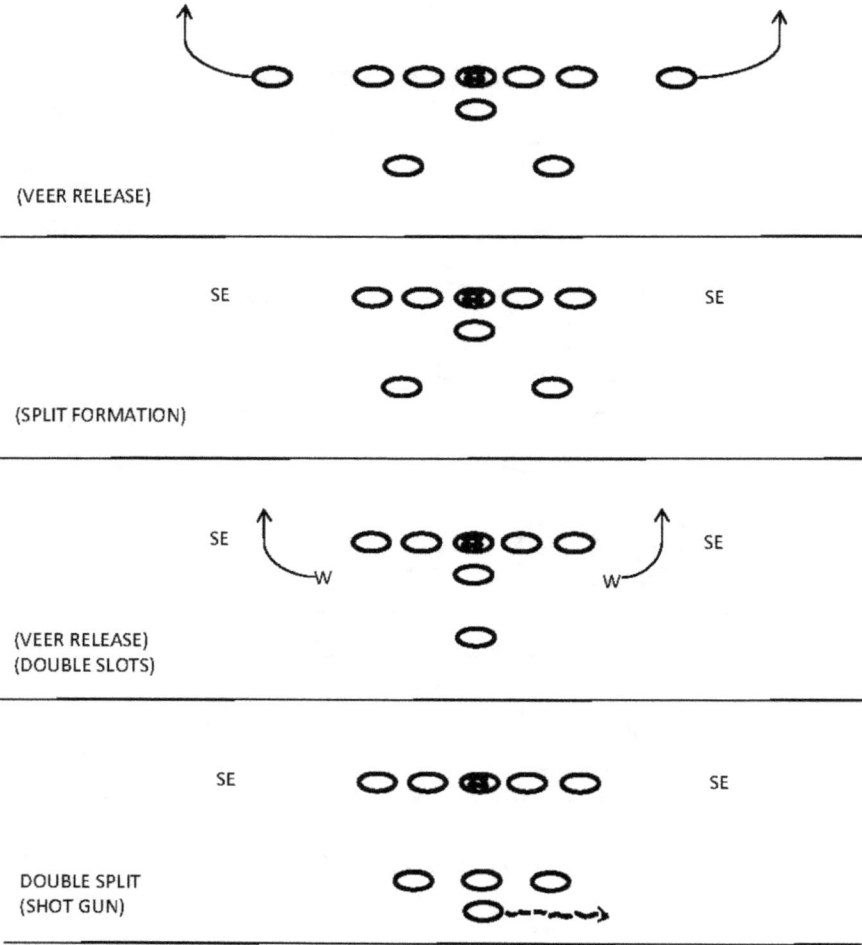

(VEER RELEASE)

SE     SE

(SPLIT FORMATION)

SE     SE

(VEER RELEASE)
(DOUBLE SLOTS)

SE     SE

DOUBLE SPLIT
(SHOT GUN)

Simple Rules to Consider: Backfield and Line

1. QB under Center or in Shotgun.
2. Fullback #No. 3, always on Tight End side of set.
3. The FB can be moved by calling "Switch."
4. The #No. 4 back is the main "motion back."
5. On a "Veer" play, the LOS will move to 3 foot splits.
6. On a "Veer" play, we do not block last man on LOS.
7. The "Tight End(s)" will release outside of the defensive player.
8. The Tight End will "flex" or widen his split at will.

# SIMPLIFYING THE QUARTERBACK'S CALLS

*(In the Huddle)*

Example: Pro Right - 214 On "Two"

1. Pro Right = Line formation
2. 2 = Backfield set
3. 1 = Blocking scheme
4. 4 = Hole number
5. On "Two" = Snap count

Example: Pro Right - 400, 646 Pass on "One"

1. Pro Right = Line formation
2. 400 = Backfield set
3. 646 = Pass routes
4. On "One" = Snap count

*(On the Line)*

1. Two words used: "Ready!" or "Check!"
2. Down!
3. Go! Go!

Note: If the linemen hear "Ready!" the play remains unchanged. If the offense hears "Check!" the quarterback can audible and change the play.

*Other quarterback calls*

1. Sprint pass - Right or left
2. Draw - Fullback or halfback

3. Boot - Right or left
4. Delay - Tight End or Wingback release
5. Motion - Action from #No. 4 back
6. Flex - Tight End widens split from tackle
7. Option - QB-Give-Keep-Pitch
8. Sweep - Halfback run or pass option

Half-Line Daily Review: Scripted (walk-throughs)

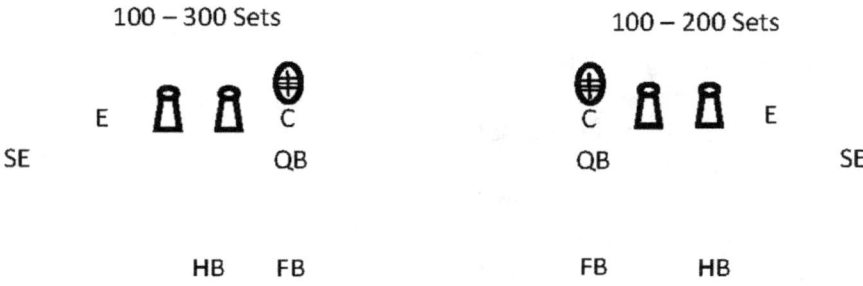

100 – 300 Sets        100 – 200 Sets

E           C           C         E

SE           QB         QB         SE

HB    FB        FB    HB

Checklist:

1. Quarterback(s) - Cadence
2. Quarterback(s) - Steps
3. Deep Hand-offs
4. Mesh/Aim Points
5. Option Reads
6. Quarterback - Center Exchange
7. Shotgun - QB snap signals

7 on 7 Passing Tree: **Daily Review**

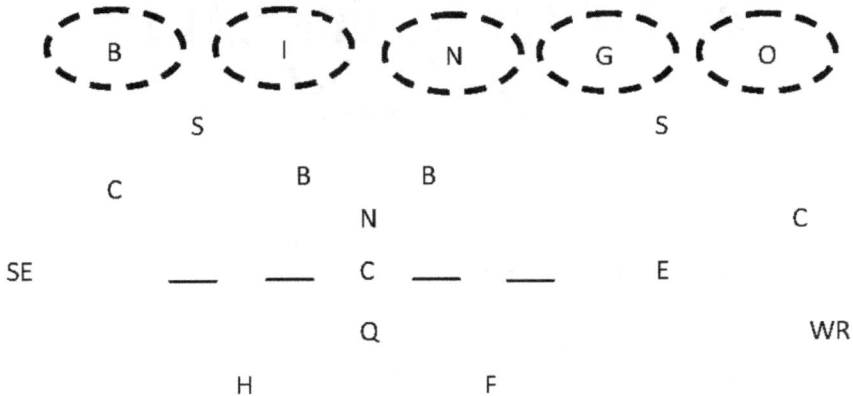

Note: Plan for the "Unexpected"

1.  2 teams of "Seven"
2.  The defense will offer a different look for each team

    A.  Cover 1, 2, 3
    B.  Zone and/or man-to-man

3.  QBs are encouraged to throw to a different receiver or back each time
4.  The "pump fake" encourages Receivers to practice an "option route"
5.  2, 3, and 4 Receiver patterns called (scripted)

# DEFENSIVE ALIGNMENTS— CHECKLIST

1. Odd/Even front = 3, 4, 5, 6 man-front
2. Linebackers - how many?
3. Secondary - zone, man, combo?
4. Who has gap responsibility?
5. Who has containment responsibility?
6. Is it a run or a pass defense?
7. Do they vary their defenses?
8. When and where do they stunt or blitz?
9. What is their short-yardage defense?
10. Who covers our motion back?

# GAME PREPARATIONS— CHECKLIST

1. QB Cards - Game plan
2. Two-minute offense (scripted)
3. Red zone offense
4. Audibles - Changing the play on the line of scrimmage
5. Automatics

   A. 5 runs
   B. 5 passes

6. Hot receivers (TE or Slot-back)
7. Wheel routes (fullback or halfback)
8. **Special plays**

   A. Read option - Veer (108-109)
   B. Draw play - QB, FB, HB
   C. Boot leg - Right and left (108-109)
   D. Toss sweep - Run or pass(208-309)
   E. Jet Sweep - Zone block (408-409)
   F. Quick Screen - Slant or hitch
   G. Sucker play series- (408-409)
   H. #No. 4 Slot-back reverse- (108-109)
   I. Tight end screen - 2 count release
   J. Shovel pass - Spread or double slot
   K. Tackle eligible - Unbalanced line
   L. Flea flicker pass- (126-127)

**Note:** These plays are best used in the second half so the other team cannot make any halftime adjustments

**Additional variations (offensive) which can be considered:**

1. QB under center - shift back
2. QB in shotgun - shift under
3. Silent snap count
4. No huddle offense
5. #No. 4 back in "motion"
6. Tight end delay - block "2" counts
7. QB throw back - 108, 109 sweep
8. Quick kick - any down

"VEER" rules reviewed – Daily = All QBs

1. Wider gaps on LOS
2. Tight end, Slot-back flex (outside release)
3. Deeper set backfield
4. QB = Deep read mesh point (60°–30°)
5. Read option, Read = Last man on LOS
6. QB = Give, keep, pitch
7. Do not block the last man on LOS

**NOTE:**

✓ Review base block rules

✓ Walk through all positions

✓ Check all defenses - odd and even sets

✓ TE-Outside release or combo on linebacker

✓ Flex technique - Tight end, wing, or slot-back

Daily Review: The Run

1. 111-110 Blast
2. 414-415 Dive
3. 127-126 Lead
4. 335-234 Belly
5. 109-108 Sweep
6. 127-126 "G"
7. 127-126 Veer (TE Flex)
8. 109-108 Dive Option
9. 109-108 Blast Option (SL/SR) (MR/ML)
10. 241-340 Trap (FB Seal Block)

Veer Optional Alignments:

Note:

- ✓ By flexing the tight end or the slot-back, "in or out" forces the defense to make new adjustments.

- ✓ By putting the slot-back in "motion" across the formation creates a one-on-one situation for the wide receiver.

- ✓ The use of a "motion back" can be used in countless ways: double team, crackback, reverses, stalk blocks, traps, and overloads in the passing game

- ✓ LOS (Wider Splits)

- ✓ Backfield (Deeper Sets)

- ✓ Tight End or Slotback (Outside Release)

# WEAKSIDE VEER (124)

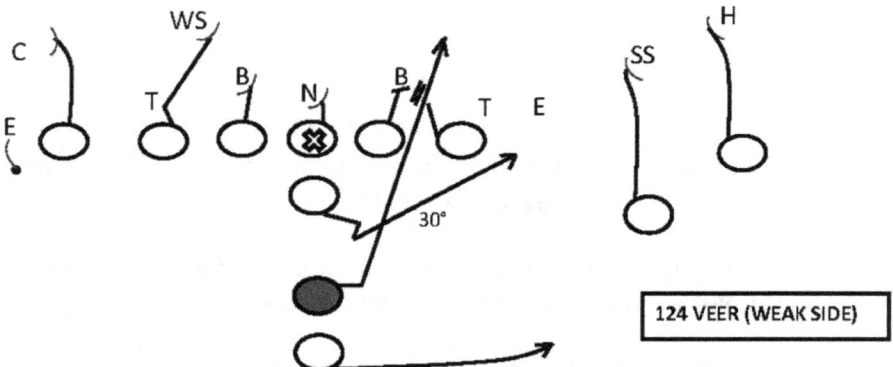

124 VEER (WEAK SIDE)

Coach's Notes:

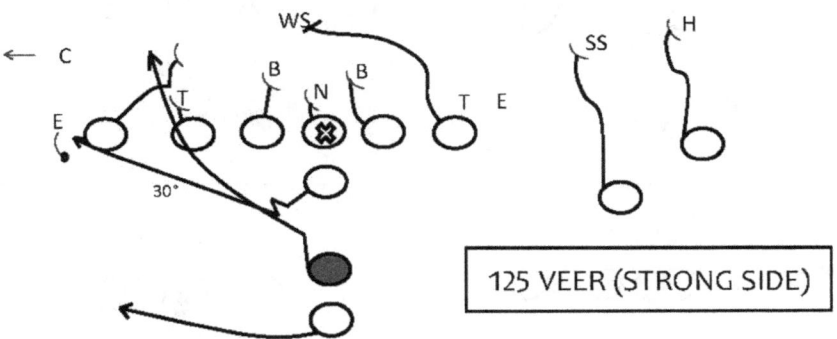

**125 VEER (STRONG SIDE)**

Coach's Notes:

# TESTING THE DEFENSIVE FRONT

## "7-Line Formations"

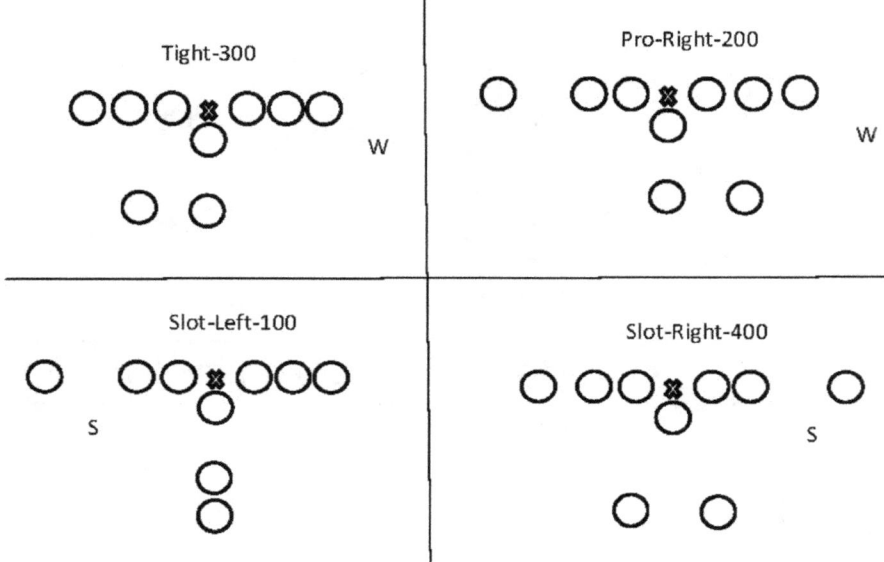

Tight-300

Pro-Right-200

Slot-Left-100

Slot-Right-400

Coach's Notes:

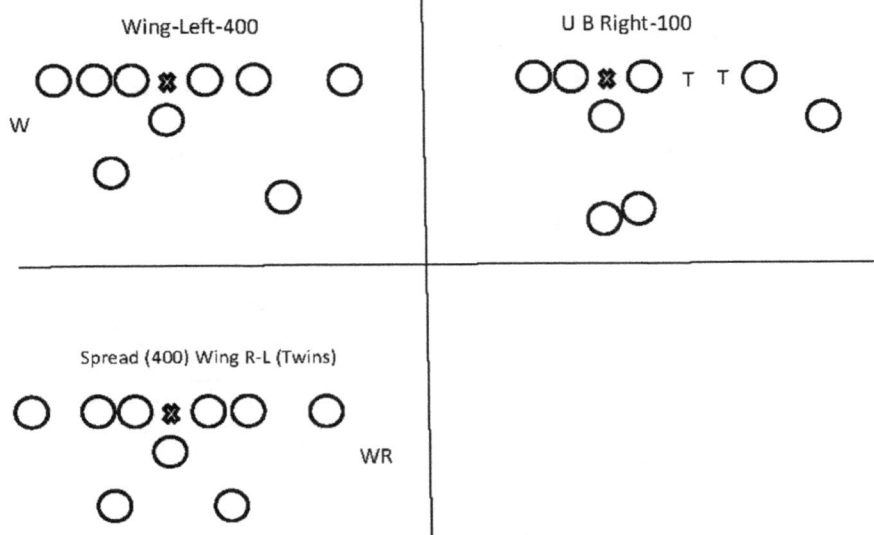

Wing-Left-400

W

U B Right-100

T   T

Spread (400) Wing R-L (Twins)

WR

Coach's Notes:

# BASE BLOCK RULES:
# ON, INSIDE, OFF, OUTSIDE

1. Option Rule - Option last man on the LOS
2. Tackle Call Rule - Inside, over, outside

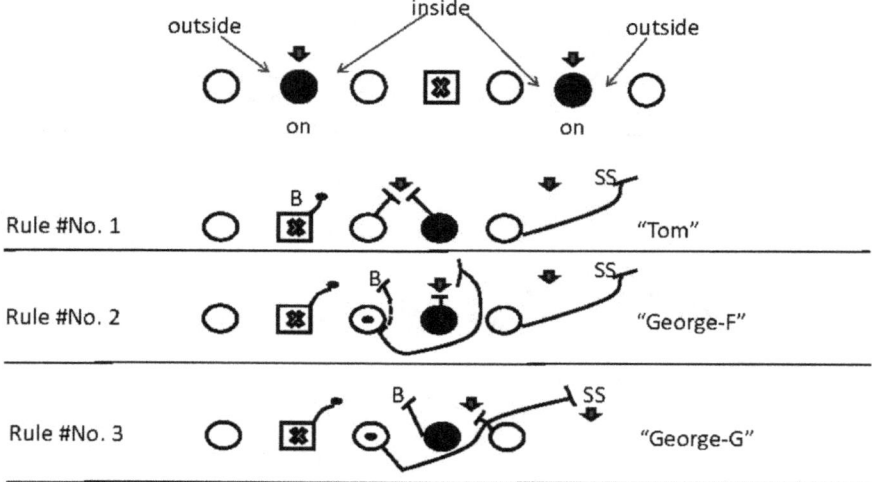

Coach's Notes:

Rule #No. 4 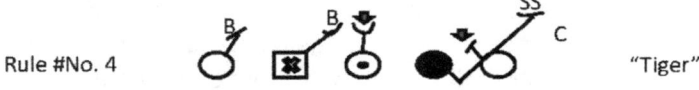 "Tiger"

**45 ° QB-OPEN STEP 45 °**

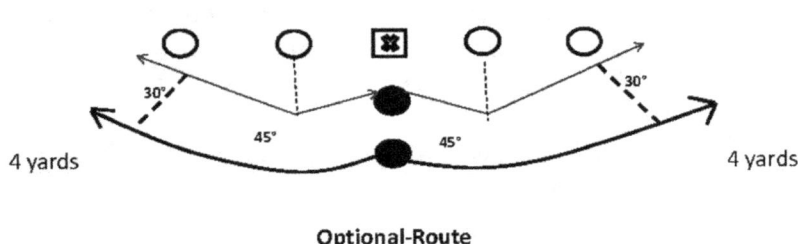

4 yards                                                                          4 yards

**Optional-Route**

Coach's Notes:

# THE PASSING GAME

In coaching, one must communicate in "terms" that are not only meaningful but also descriptive and concise. These "code words," along with the numbers 1 through 8 and 0, will be necessary in the development of a "passing game package." In the daily teaching phase, the coach and the player learn to communicate in "code words" that will develop into a language of football terms that become second nature to both the teacher and the learner.

Many terms or code words listed here are only suggestions. These words are used by other coaches and by no means limit the communication but simplify it. Some examples are *motion, stop and go, sideline, option route, comeback, outlet, back shoulder, pump fake, hitch, check, screen, spot, delay, wheel, hot receiver*, etc.

The next set of terms involves the quarterback that indicates his action in executing a "pass play":

1. Drop Back - 3, 5, or 7 steps
2. Sprint Out - right or left
3. Play Action - base block, play-side
4. Boot Leg - QB misdirection
5. Shotgun - "5" yards from the ball set

# THE PASSING TREE

After many years of experimenting with many systems using the usual code words, such as *sideline*, *flag*, *post*, and others, I decided on substituting numbers into the passing game to cover the basic pass routes. With a few rules and/or modifications to fit one's needs, a strong passing game can be adopted and realized.

Passing Tree Rules: Quarterback Calls

1. All receivers have the same numbers.
2. Odd numbers (1, 3, 5, 7) go to the left.
3. Even numbers (2, 4, 6, 8) go to the right.
4. On all offensive sets with 2, 3, or 4 possible receivers, the number called will be read from left to right.
5. If the number 0 is included by the quarterback, that receiver will stay and pass block.

The Passing Game: Quarterback Action

1. Drop back pass - 3, 5, 7 steps
2. Sprint right or left pass
3. Play action pass - blast or dive action
4. Boot leg - right or left (Tight End delay pass)
5. Screens - right, middle, or left
6. Shotgun set - 4 possible receivers

# OFFENSIVE SCHEMES (THE PASS)

| 1 RECEIVER SIDE | 2 RECEIVER SIDE |
|---|---|

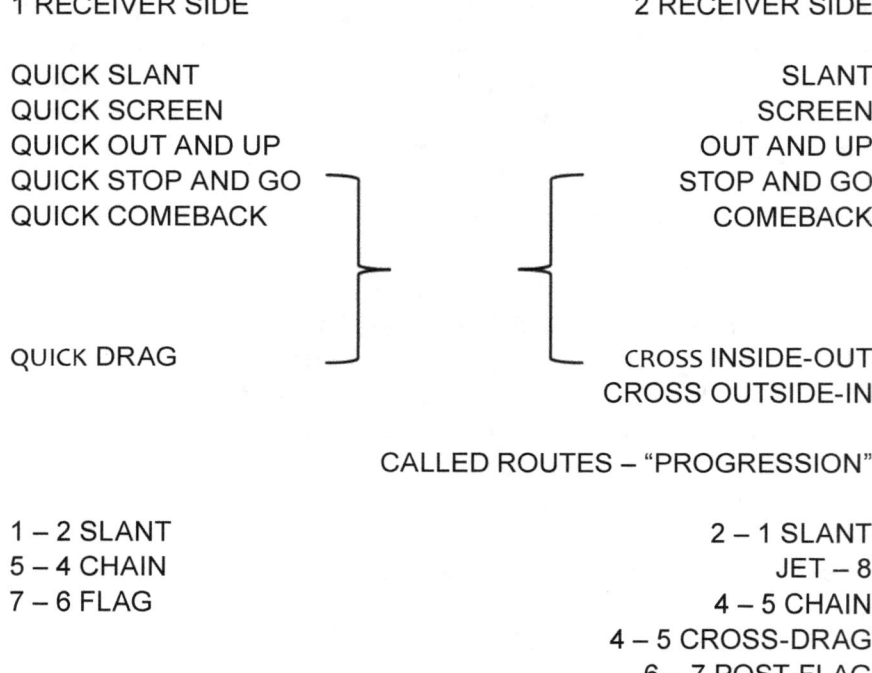

| 1 RECEIVER SIDE | 2 RECEIVER SIDE |
|---|---|
| QUICK SLANT | SLANT |
| QUICK SCREEN | SCREEN |
| QUICK OUT AND UP | OUT AND UP |
| QUICK STOP AND GO | STOP AND GO |
| QUICK COMEBACK | COMEBACK |
| QUICK DRAG | CROSS INSIDE-OUT |
| | CROSS OUTSIDE-IN |

CALLED ROUTES – "PROGRESSION"

| | |
|---|---|
| 1 – 2 SLANT | 2 – 1 SLANT |
| 5 – 4 CHAIN | JET – 8 |
| 7 – 6 FLAG | 4 – 5 CHAIN |
| | 4 – 5 CROSS-DRAG |
| | 6 – 7 POST-FLAG |

## Four Receivers

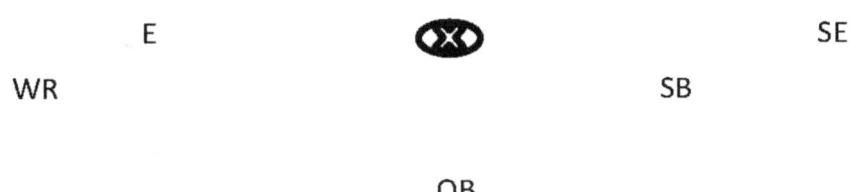

## The Passing Tree: For 2, 3, 4, or 5 Receivers

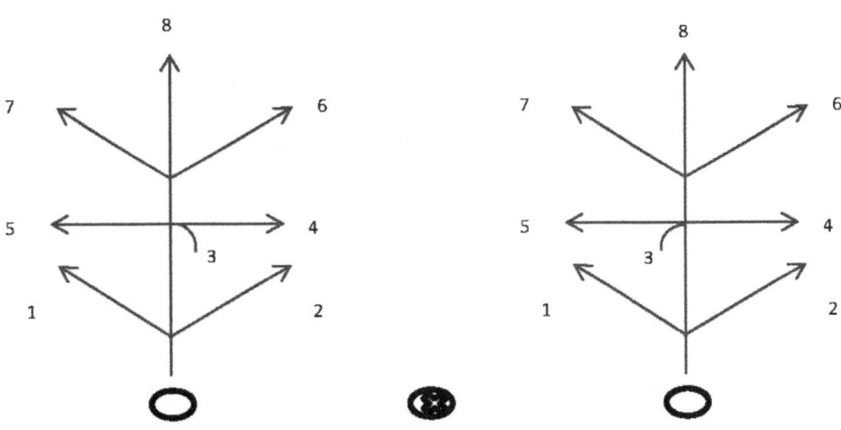

## Five Possible Receivers
### 865

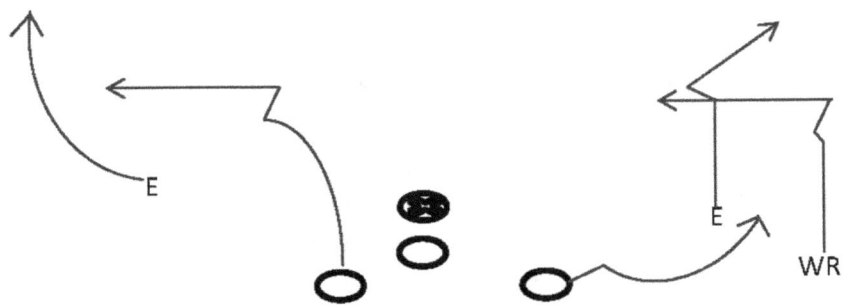

Coach's Notes:

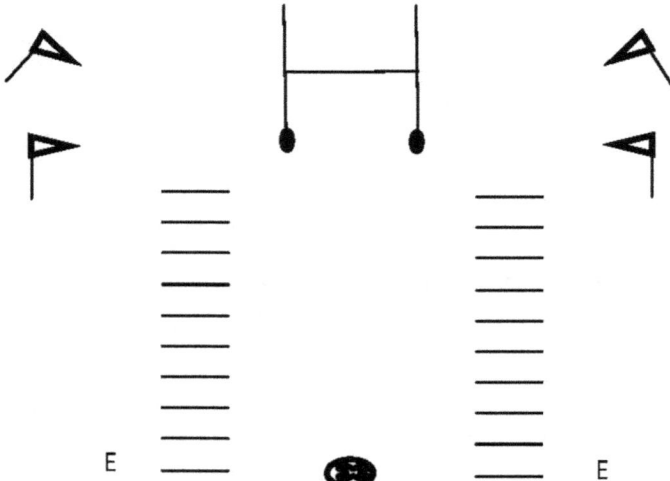

E                                    E

Commonly used football terms:

1. L.O.S.
2. Corner
3. Flag
4. Post
5. Chain
6. Hash marks
7. Sideline
8. Drag
9. Shotgun
10. Motion
11. Flex
12. Reverse
13. Split End
14. Wide Receiver

15. Twins
16. Trips
17. Slot
18. Wing
19. Delay
20. Seal Block
21. Combo
22. Lead
23. Load
24. Wheel
25. Victory
26. Blitz
27. Scramble
28. Pump Fake

Introducing an Offensive System:

1. Classroom- playbook
2. Line of scrimmage- hole numbering system
3. Backs- numbers by position
4. Backfield sets- 100, 200, 300, 400
5. The huddle
6. Quarterback calls: The run

   A. Formation (code word)
   B. Blocking scheme
   C. Hole number
   D. Snap count

Communication-Progression-Execution

1. On the field- review
2. Quarterback

   A. Under center- ball exchanges
   B. Steps- mesh points
   C. Give or keep reads
   D. Finish the play- Good Fakes!
   E. Check quarterback to trail-back separation

3. Backfield sets- Fullback and halfback

   A. Distance from the ball (5 yards)
   B. 3 point stance
   C. Aim points- step angles

4. #4 Back is the "motion back" on all sets

   A. Wide receiver, wing or slot-back
   B. Blocker, runner, passer, decoy

# Half Line Offense: Dive Series versus Odd / Even Defense

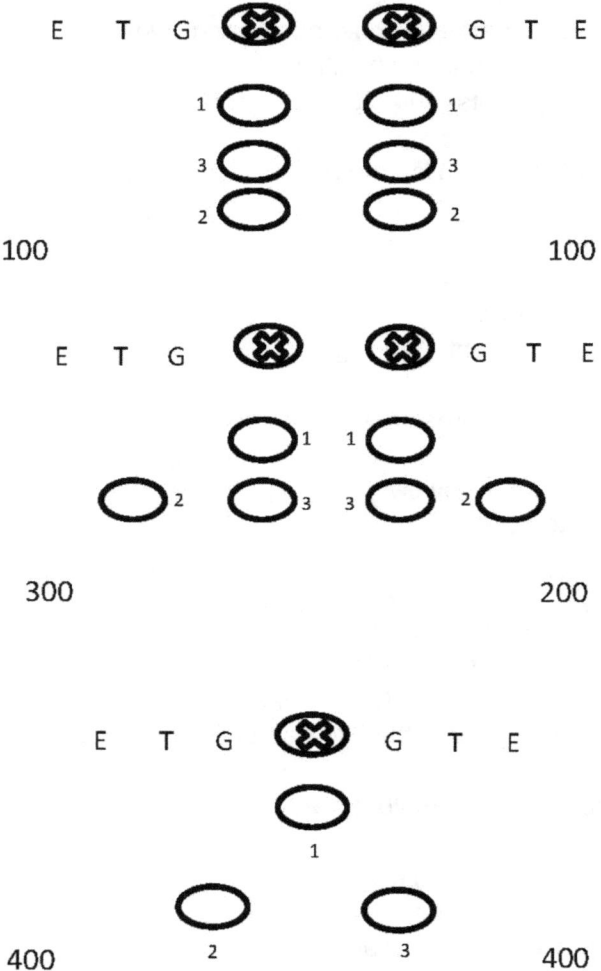

5. Screens- right, middle, or left

6. Shotgun set - 4 possible receivers

Coach's Notes:

## Three Receivers

## Four Receivers

## Three Receivers

Coach's Notes:

These "2" plays are practiced daily as warm-up for all backs and receivers versus zone or man to man secondary

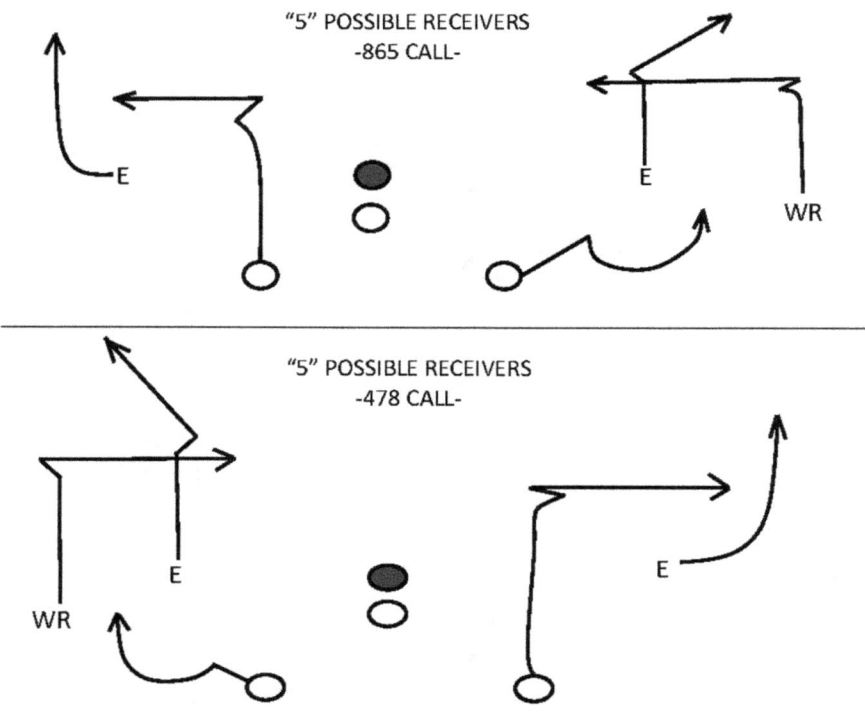

"5" POSSIBLE RECEIVERS
-865 CALL-

"5" POSSIBLE RECEIVERS
-478 CALL-

"3" simple rules for "option" routes

1. QB = Pump Fakes
2. Zone Drop = Stop Routes
3. Man Coverage = Cross Routes, Slants

Coach's Notes

# DAILY REVIEW: THE PASS (MAN/ZONE/BUMP-RUN)

1. Quick Slant  =  #No. 1, #No. 2 Routes
2. Hot Pass  =  Tight End, Slot-back
3. Check Pass  =  #No. 2, #No. 3 Backs - Swing Route
4. Hitch Pass  =  Wide Outs (Comebacks)
5. Slot Screen  =  Shovel Pass
6. TE Screen  =  Comeback - Zone Block
7. HB Pass  =  Middle, Stop, Go (638)
8. HB-FB Dive  =  Dive Rule Blocks

NOTE: 2, 5, 7 Step Drop, 2–3 Second Release

# QUARTERBACK AND RECEIVERS: VISUAL KEYS

1. Zone Reads
2. Man-to-Man Reads
3. Sideline Rule (5 yards)
4. Using the Hash marks
5. Using the Numbers on the field

| QBs = 3 Step drop | Receivers = 3 yards |
| --- | --- |
| 5 Step drop | 7 yards |
| 7 Step drop | 10 yards |

On Spot Passes

1. Throw to Hash marks
2. Throw to Numbers
3. Throw to Sideline

QBs and receivers: Visually both READ and REACT to Man coverage or zone coverage:

Note:

In this drill, no numbers or pass patterns are called. If the receiver is *on* the numbers or hash marks, he is signaling to the QB that he is going deep; but if the defender backs up, the receiver runs a stop route, spins, and shows his numbers to the QB at ten to twelve yards. With repetition and timing, the QB can deliver the ball to the receiver as he (the receiver) anticipates that the ball is there immediately.

The next maneuver to the stop drill is for the receiver to fake the stop and add a stop-and-go maneuver.

Two other variations to this drill are for the receiver to line up outside the numbers or the hash marks and *fake out* and take an inside pass maneuver. The next maneuver is to line up inside the hash mark or field numbers and *fake* an *inside move* and go outside.

The QB and Receivers - Coordinating Reads

1.  Receivers
    A. Quick release of LOS
    B. Elude the defender
    C. Bull Rush - 2 hand shiver
    D. Arm Bar - forearm bar
    E. Good-Quick footwork

2.  Run precise pass routes
    A. Short Routes      3–5 yards
    B. Medium Routes     7–10 yards
    C. Deep Routes       12–15 yards

3.  Read the defender (keys)
    A. Tight Coverage (outside release)
    B. Loose Coverage (inside slants)
    C. Inside Shade (man-to-man)
    D. Outside Shade (zone cover-Funnel in)

4.  Using the Field Markings (visuals)
    A. Sideline Rule: 5 yards, minimum
    B. Hash marks - In-On-Outside
    C. Field Numbers - In-On-Outside
    D. Stop Routes - Hook or Curl
    E. Comeback Routes - Low throws
    F. Back Shoulder Throws - Toward sideline

Coach's Note: Simple Rules for QBs and Receivers

Quarterback

1.  Defensive secondary coverages.
2.  Work on quick releases.

3. Work on pass progressions.
4. Lead your receivers.
5. Throw away from nearest defender.
6. If no receiver is open, "throw it away."

Receivers

1. Run precise routes.
2. Get quick separation.
3. Catch the ball at its highest point.
4. Eyes on the ball, two hands on the ball.
5. Secure the ball after the catch.

**DIVE**

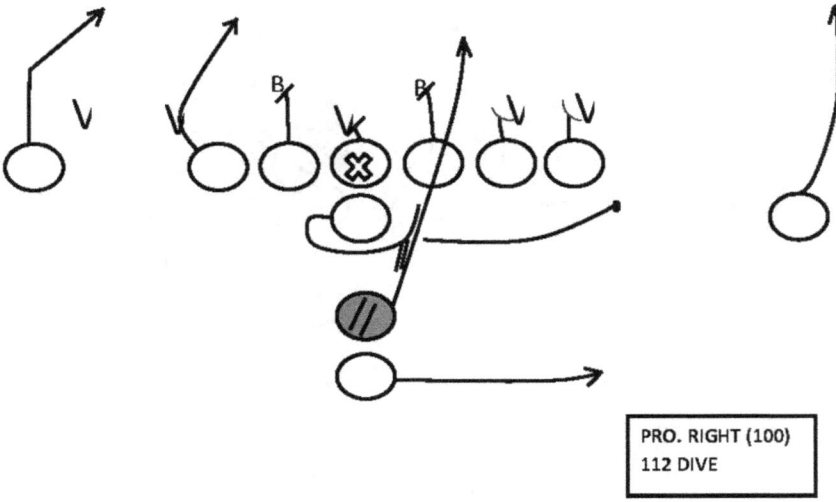

PRO. RIGHT (100)
112 DIVE

Coach's Note:

1)

2)

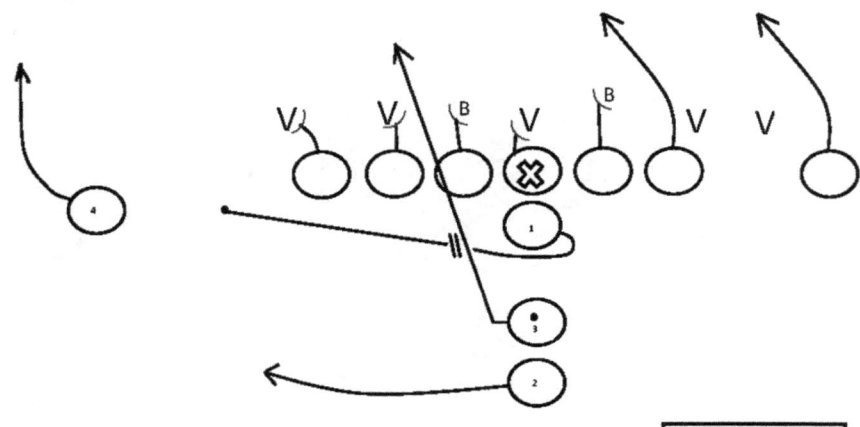

PRO. LEFT (100)
113 DIVE = 119 DIVE
OPTION

(VEER)

INSIDE VEER
OPTION

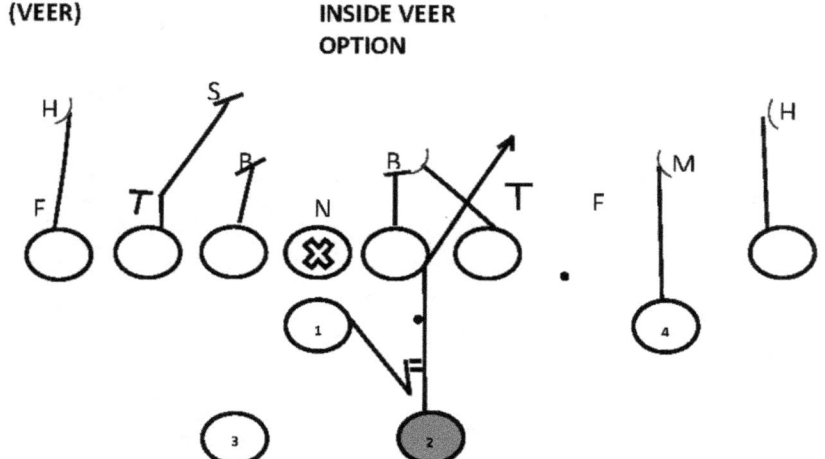

Coach's Notes:

(SLOT RT. 400)
414 VEER

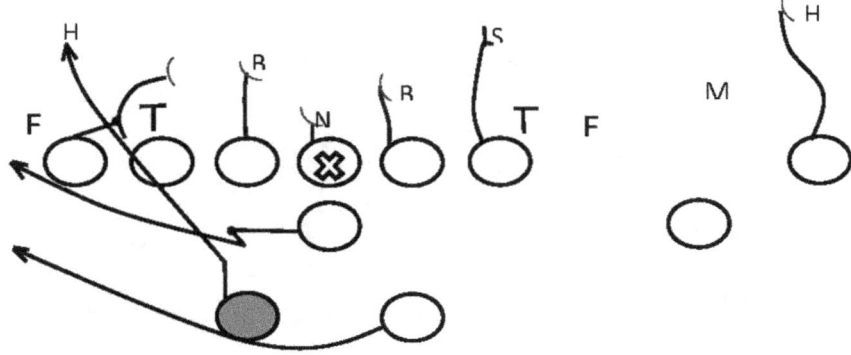

Coach's Notes:

> SLOT RIGHT-400
> 425 GIVE

**BLAST**

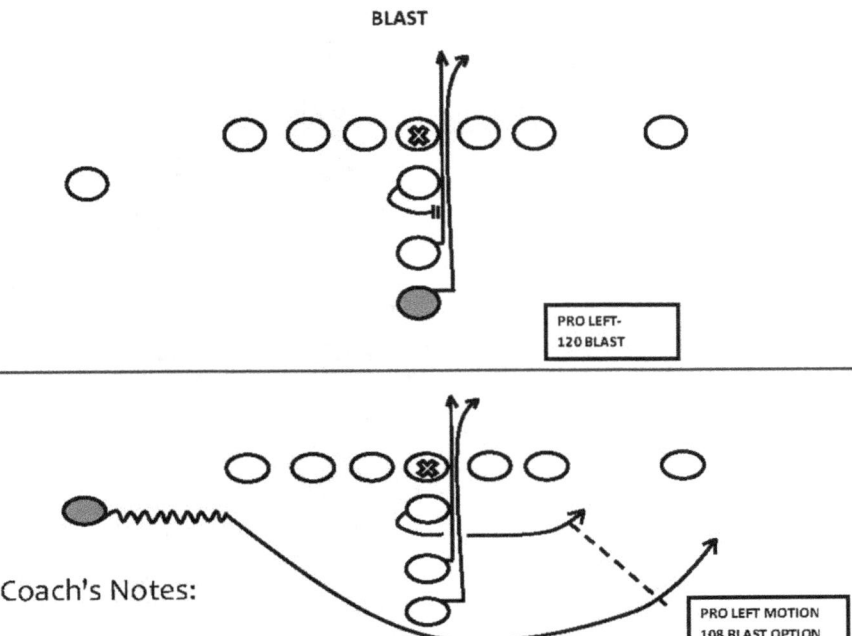

> PRO LEFT-
> 120 BLAST

Coach's Notes:

> PRO LEFT MOTION
> 108 BLAST OPTION

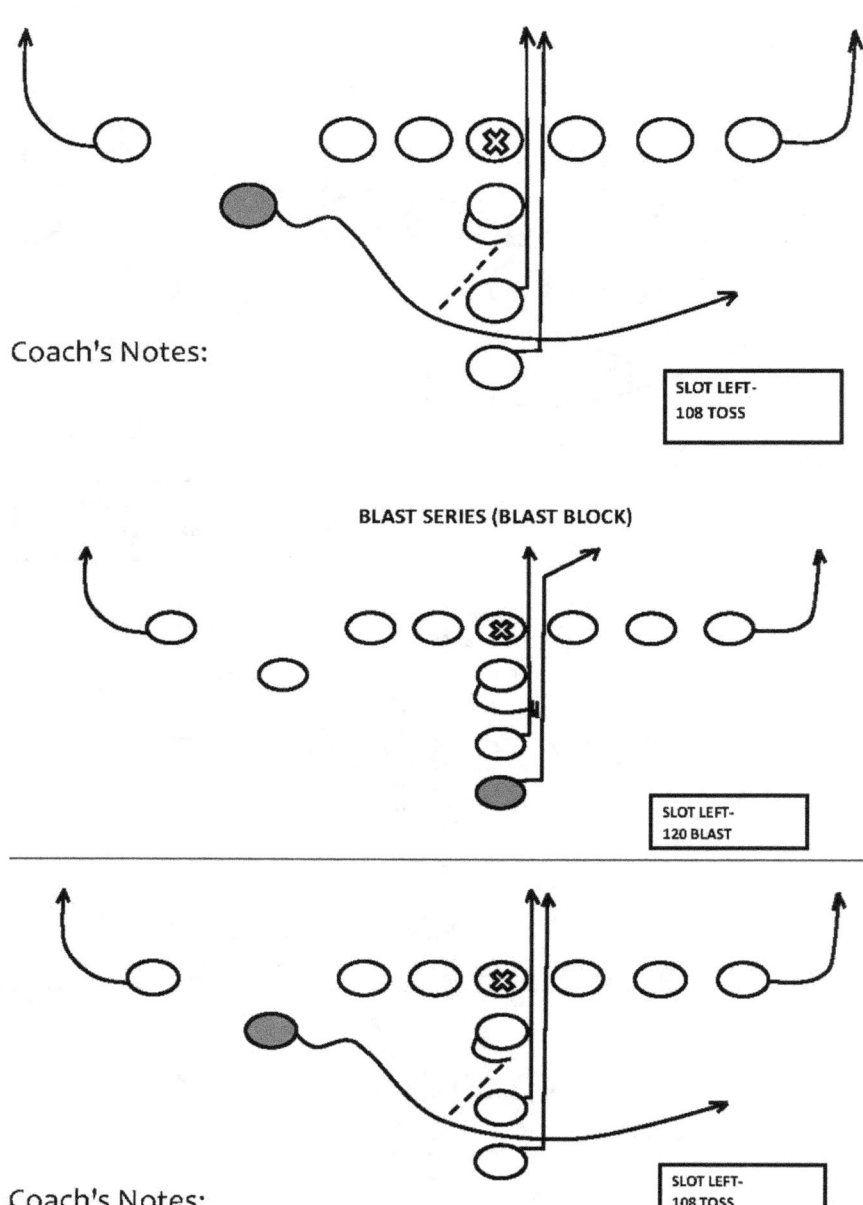

Coach's Notes:

SLOT LEFT-
108 TOSS

**BLAST SERIES (BLAST BLOCK)**

SLOT LEFT-
120 BLAST

Coach's Notes:

SLOT LEFT-
108 TOSS

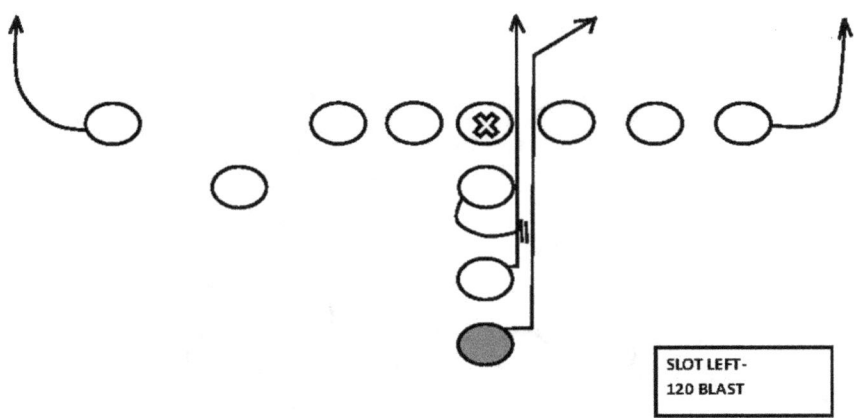

**BLAST SERIES (BLAST BLOCK)**

SLOT LEFT-
120 BLAST

Coach's Notes:

1. Rule Block

2. Double Team NG

**BLAST SERIES**

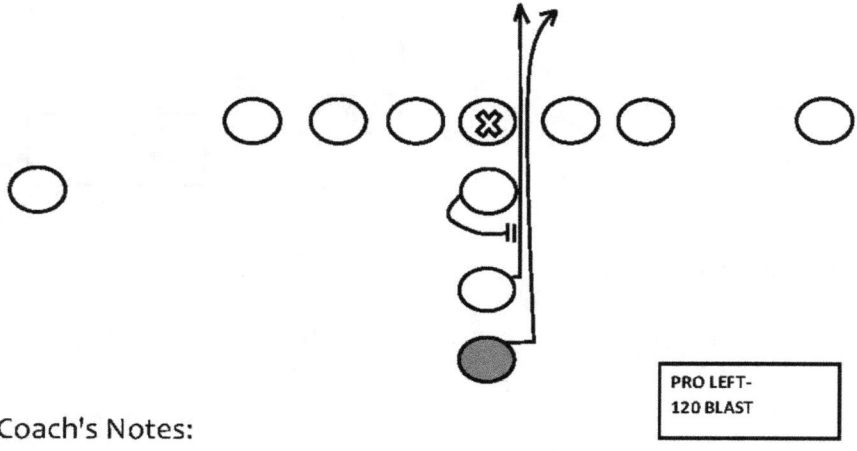

PRO LEFT-
120 BLAST

Coach's Notes:

Coach's Notes:

## Blast Series (ISO-Linebacker)

Blast Series (ISO-Linebacker)

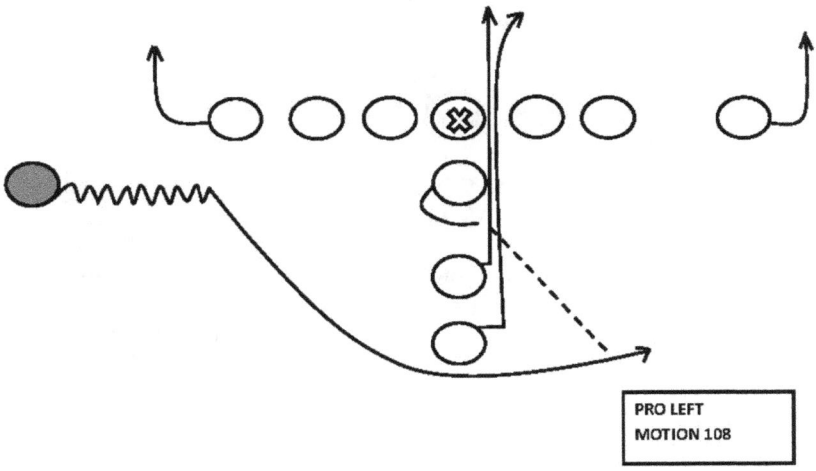

PRO LEFT
MOTION 108

Coach's note:

1. Flip 109

2. Slot RT. 109

**BLAST SERIES**

DT-NOSEGUARD

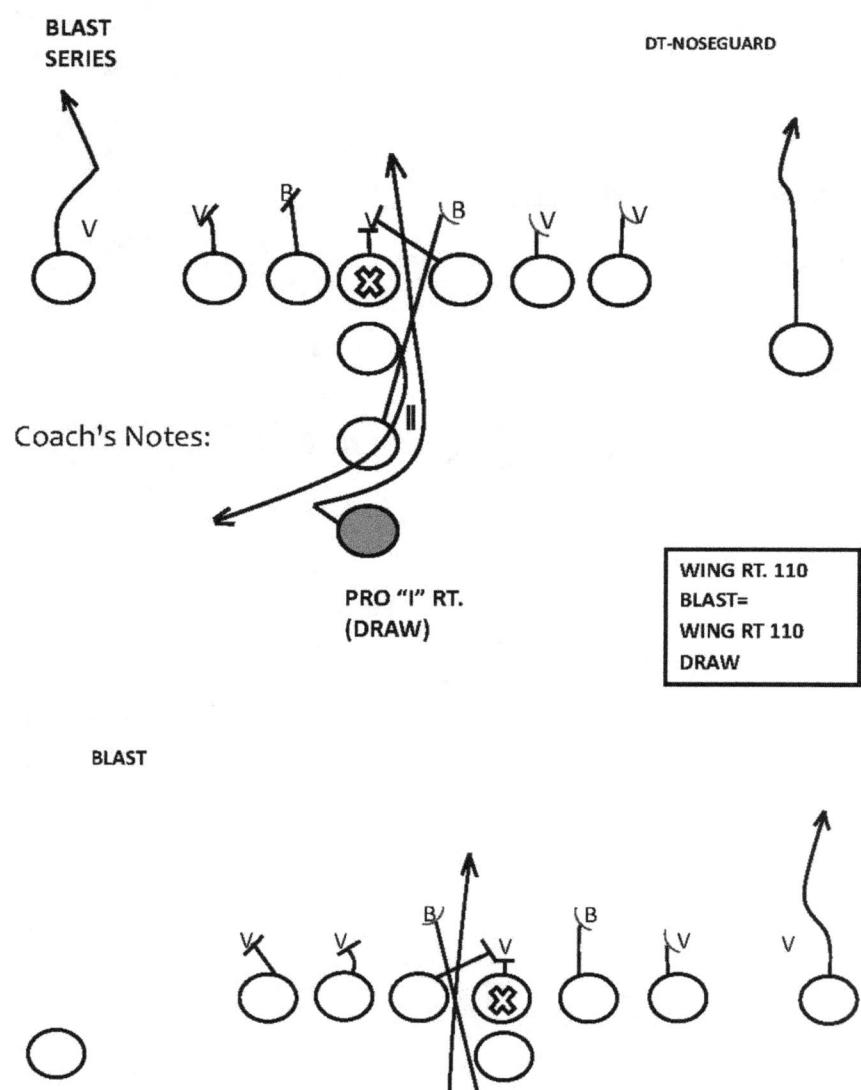

Coach's Notes:

PRO "I" RT.
(DRAW)

WING RT. 110
BLAST=
WING RT 110
DRAW

**BLAST**

Coach's Notes:

DOUBLE TEAM-

PRO. LEFT-100
111 BLAST

**BLAST PASS**

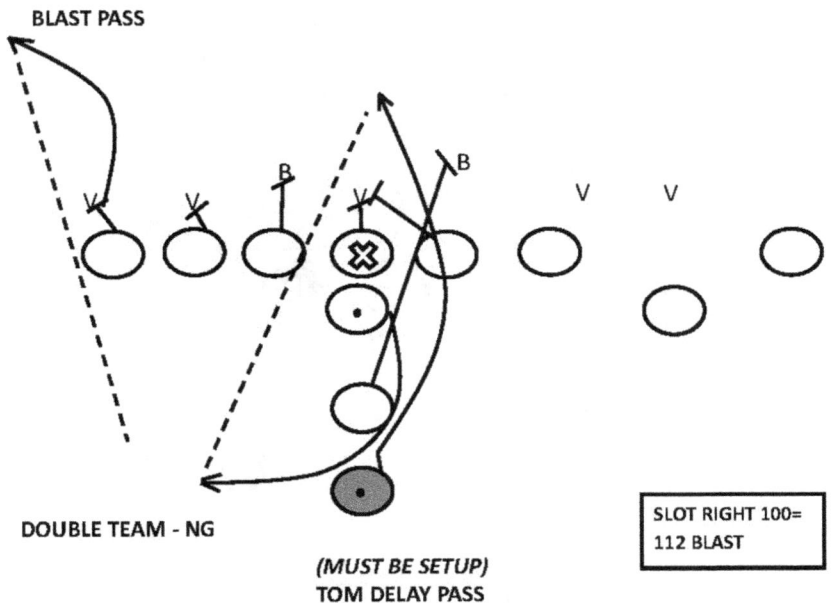

**DOUBLE TEAM - NG**

*(MUST BE SETUP)*
**TOM DELAY PASS**

**SLOT RIGHT 100=
112 BLAST**

Coach's Note:

**BLAST SERIES**

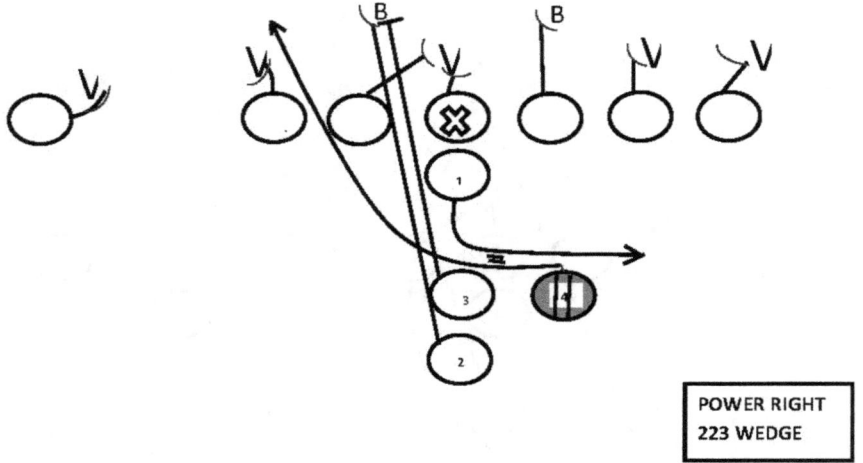

POWER RIGHT
223 WEDGE

Coach's Note:

1. Stack 200 Formation

2. Veer 208 Keeper

**BLAST SERIES**

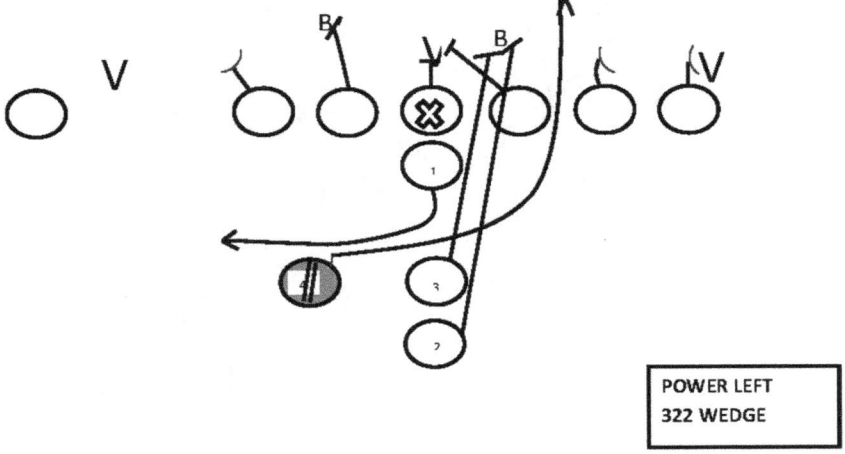

POWER LEFT
322 WEDGE

Coach's Notes:

1. Stack 300 Formation

2. Naked Boot Left

# BLAST SERIES

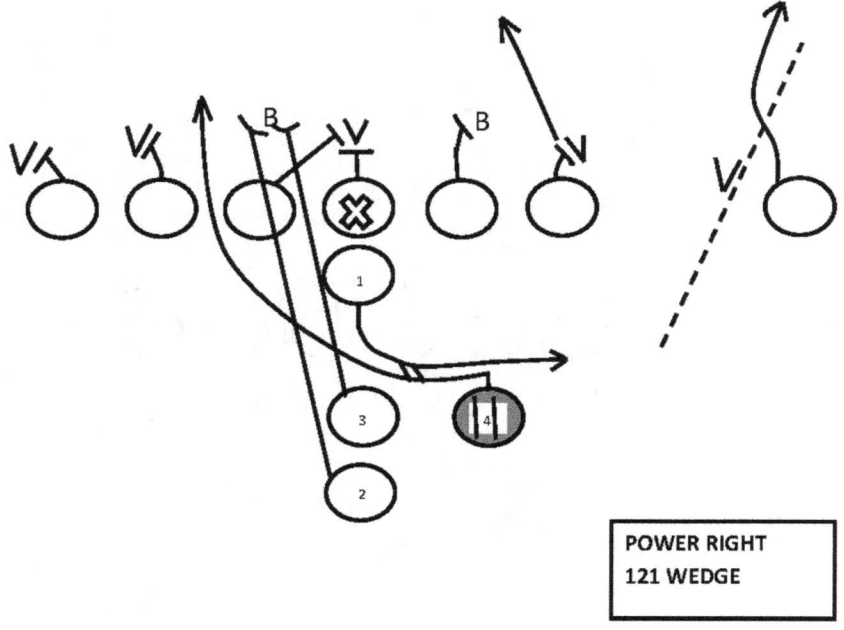

**POWER RIGHT**
**121 WEDGE**

Coach's Note:

1. Stack 200 Formation

2. WR-Delay Decoy

## BELLY
## SERIES

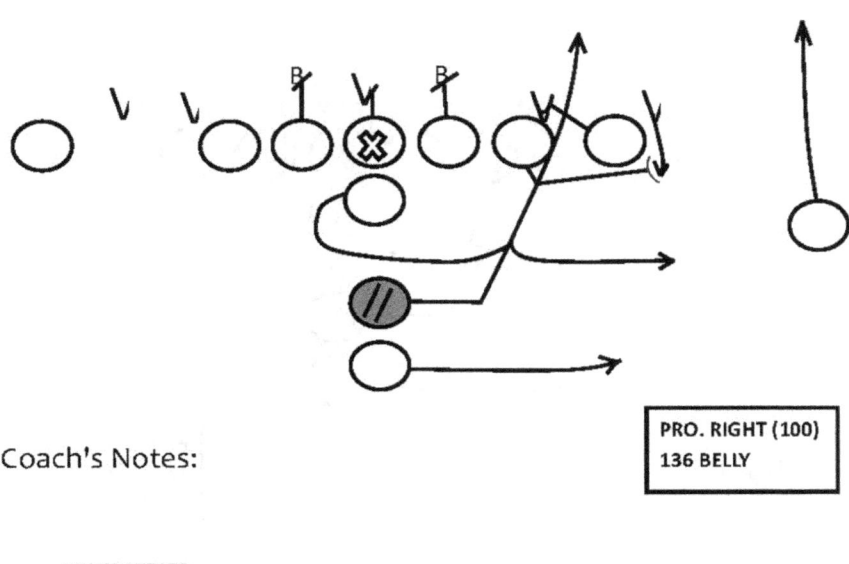

**Coach's Notes:**

PRO. RIGHT (100)
136 BELLY

## BELLY SERIES

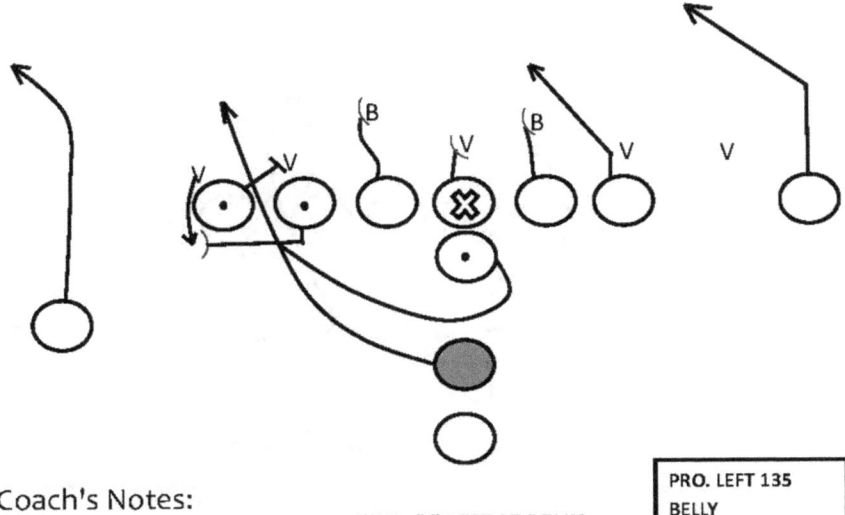

**Coach's Notes:**

PRO. "I" LEFT 17 BELLY

PRO. LEFT 135
BELLY

## BELLY

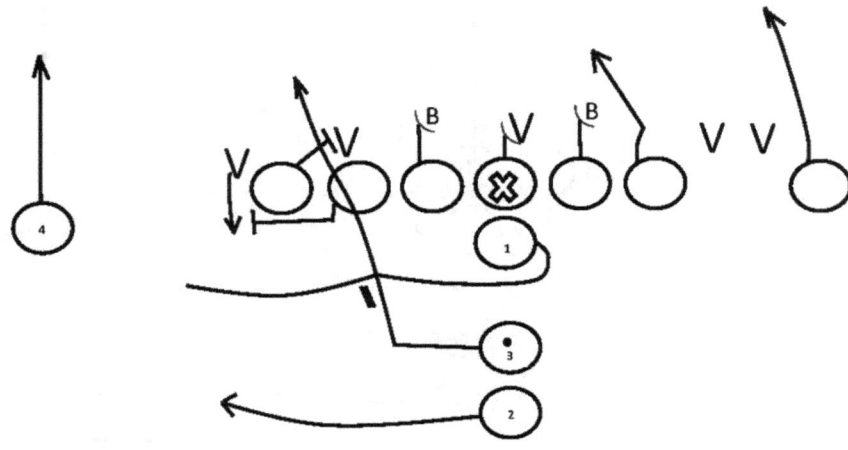

**Coach's Notes:**

PRO. LEFT (100)
135 BELLY = 109
BELLY OPTION

## BELLY SERIES

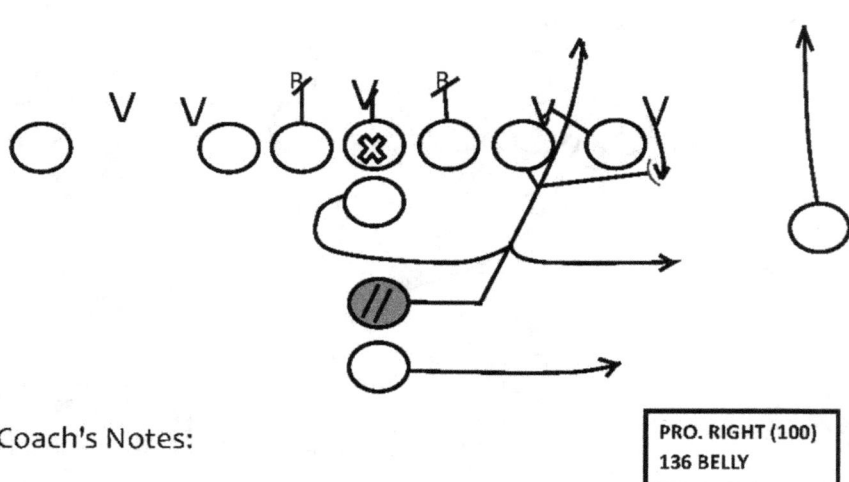

**Coach's Notes:**

PRO. RIGHT (100)
136 BELLY

## LEAD SERIES

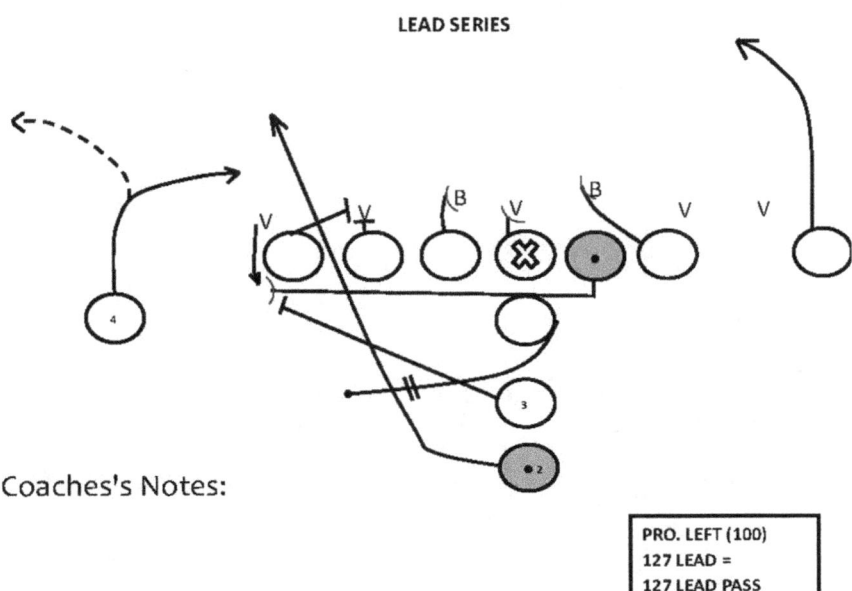

**Coaches's Notes:**

PRO. LEFT (100)
127 LEAD =
127 LEAD PASS

---

**(VEER)**          **VEER LEAD OPTION**

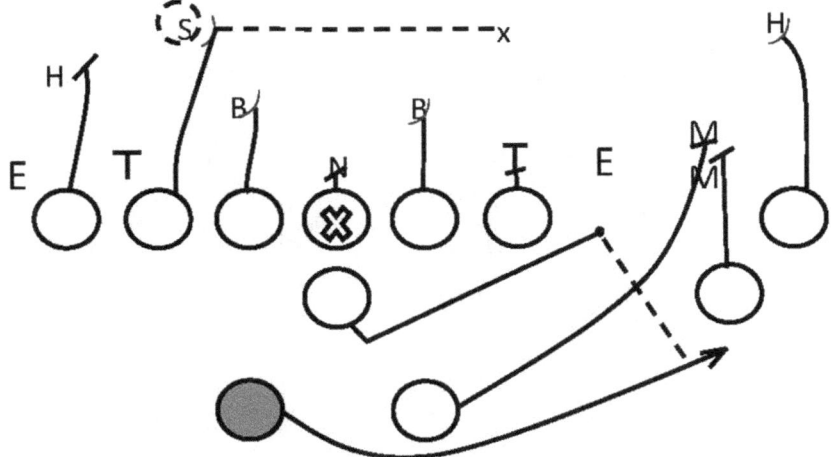

**Coaches's Notes:**

408 LEAD
OPTION

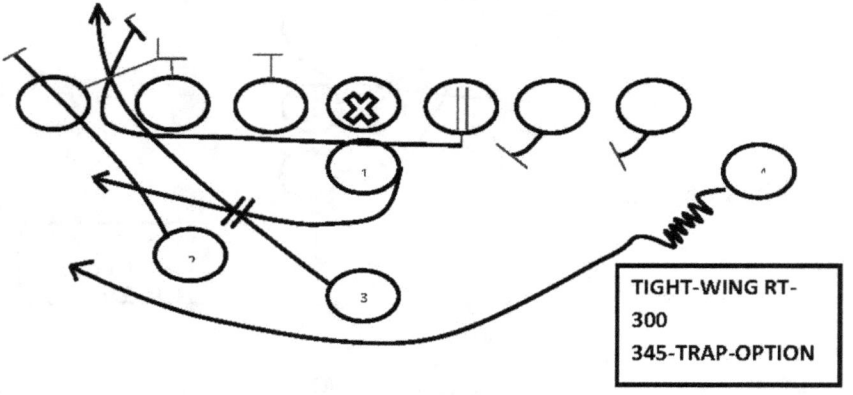

TIGHT-WING RT-
300
345-TRAP-OPTION

Coach's Note:

1. Two Tight Ends

# TRAP SERIES

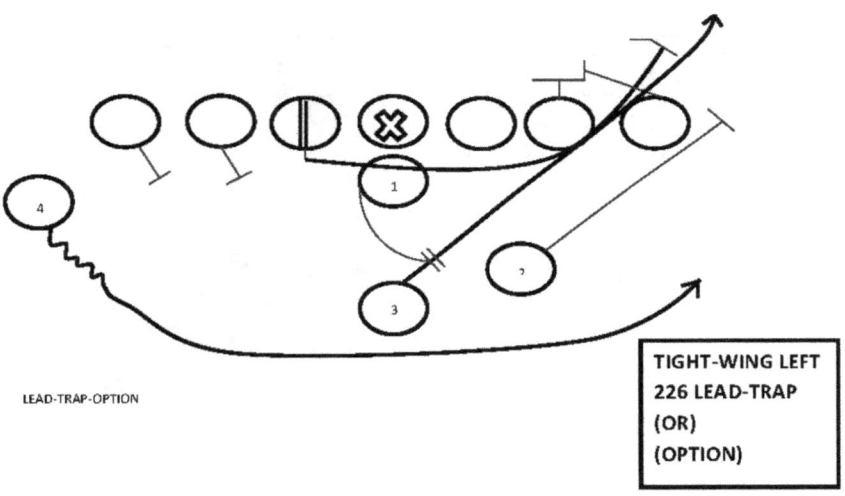

LEAD-TRAP-OPTION

**TIGHT-WING LEFT**
**226 LEAD-TRAP**
**(OR)**
**(OPTION)**

Coach's Notes:

# TRAP SERIES

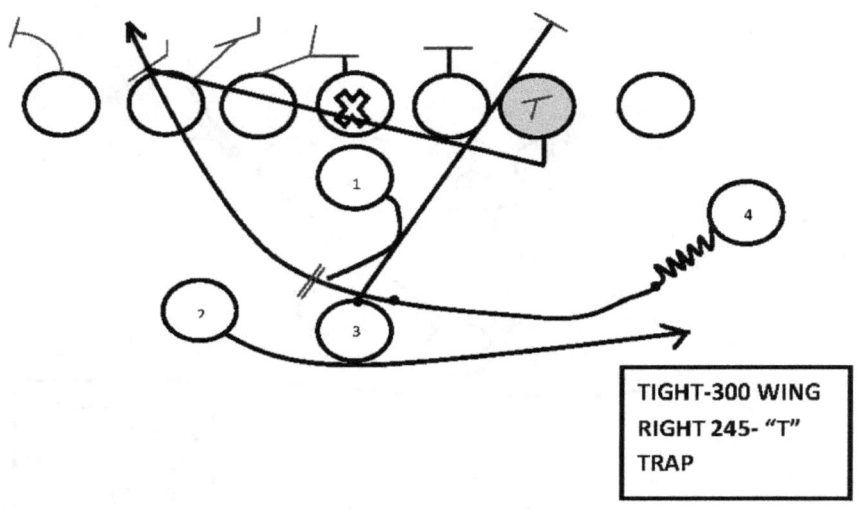

TIGHT-300 WING
RIGHT 245- "T"
TRAP

Coach's Note:

1.  Wing #No. 4 BACK TRAP

# TRAP SERIES

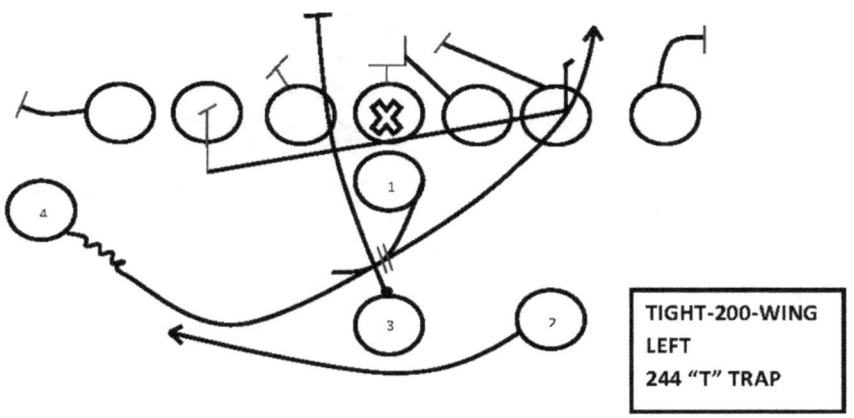

TIGHT-200-WING
LEFT
244 "T" TRAP

Coach's Note:

1. Pro Left

2. Slot Left

# TRAP SERIES

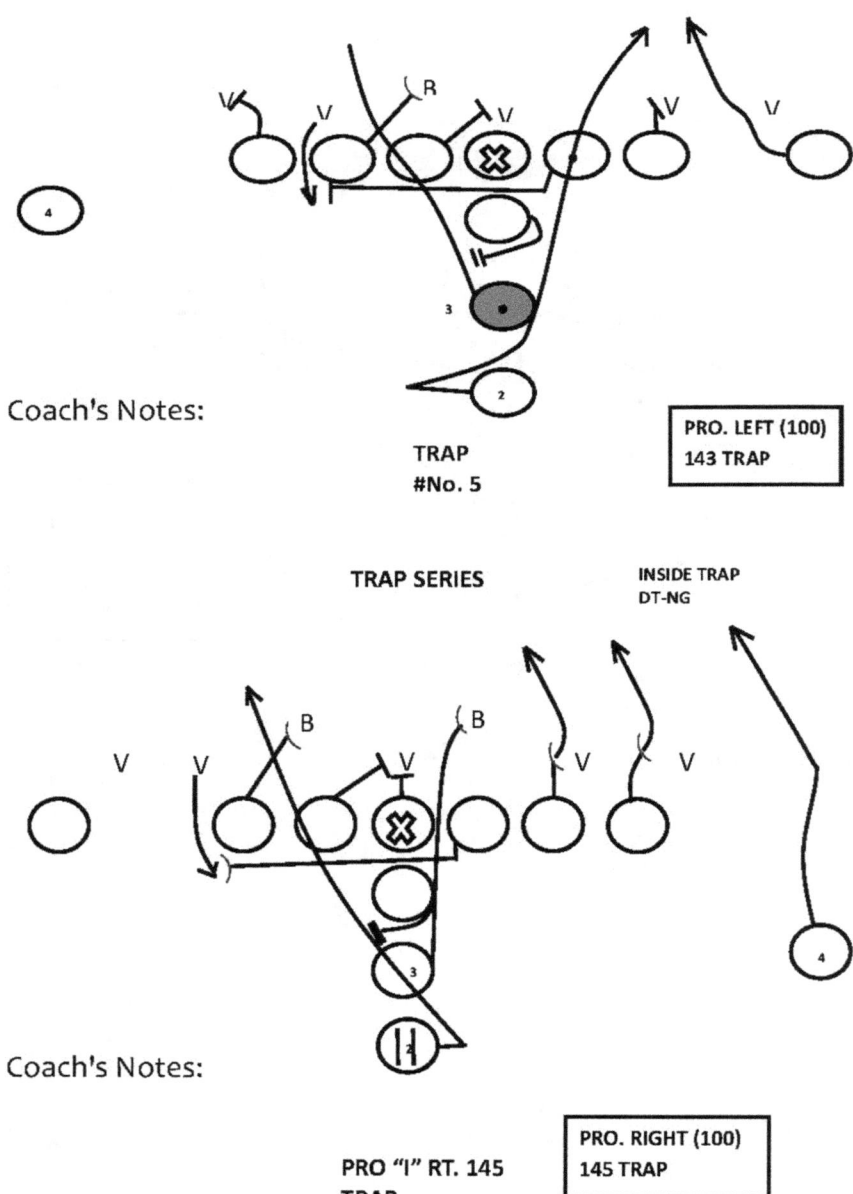

Coach's Notes:

TRAP
#No. 5

PRO. LEFT (100)
143 TRAP

**TRAP SERIES**

INSIDE TRAP
DT-NG

Coach's Notes:

PRO "I" RT. 145
TRAP

PRO. RIGHT (100)
145 TRAP

# TRAP SERIES

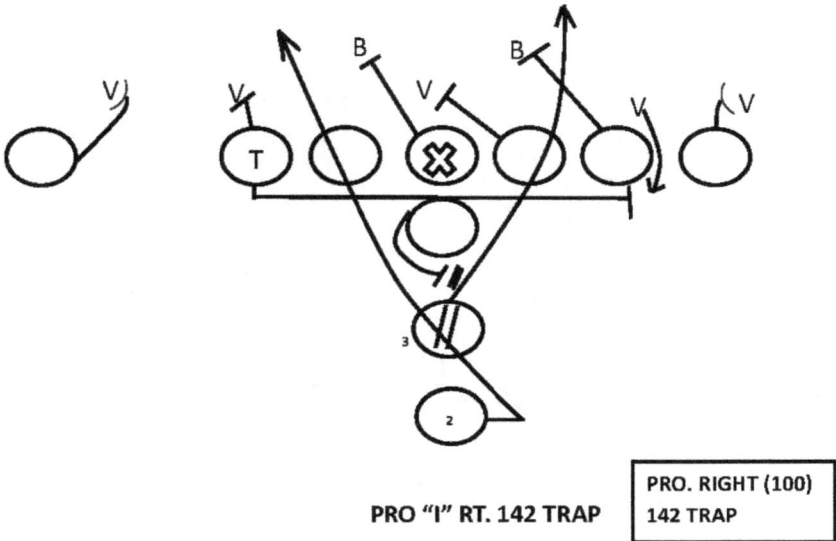

**PRO "I" RT. 142 TRAP**

| PRO. RIGHT (100) |
| 142 TRAP |

Coach's Notes:

## Weak Side Trap

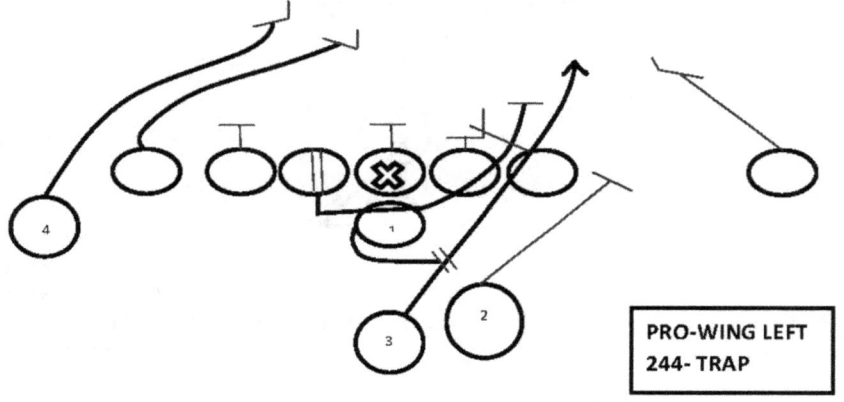

PRO-WING LEFT
244- TRAP

Coach's Note:

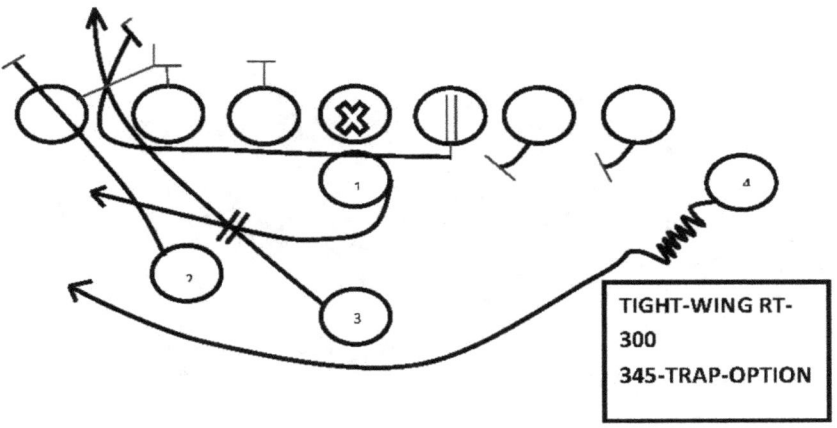

Coach's Note:

1. Halfback Trap

# Trap Series Specials

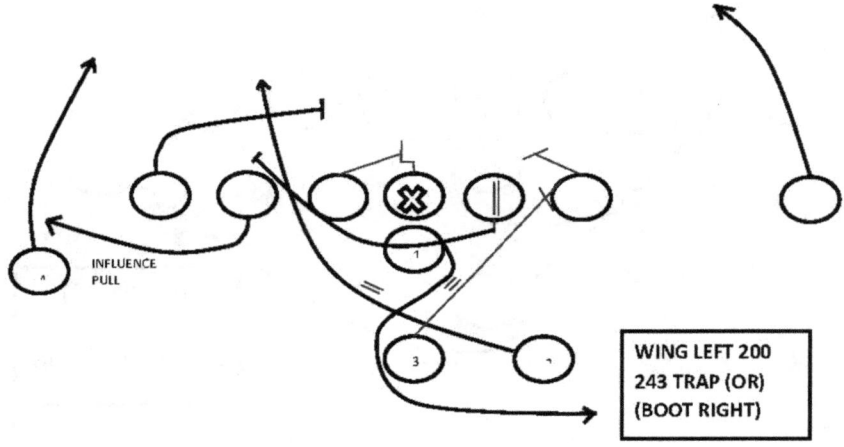

INFLUENCE
PULL

WING LEFT 200
243 TRAP (OR)
(BOOT RIGHT)

Coach's Note:

1. Halfback Trap

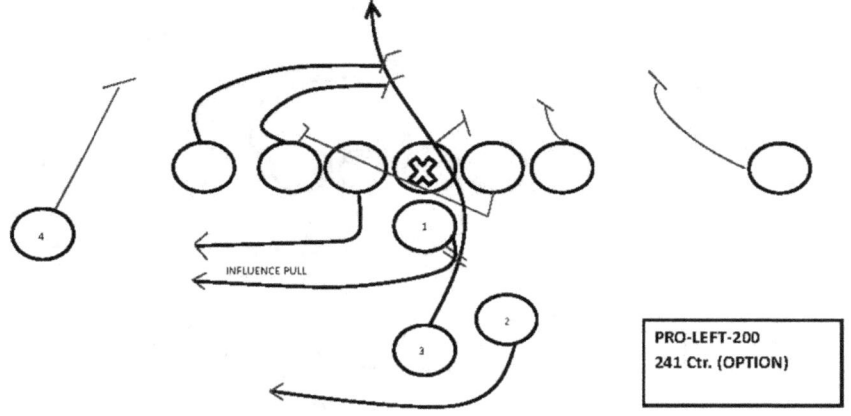

PRO-LEFT-200
241 Ctr. (OPTION)

INFLUENCE PULL

Coach's Note:

1. Fullback Trap

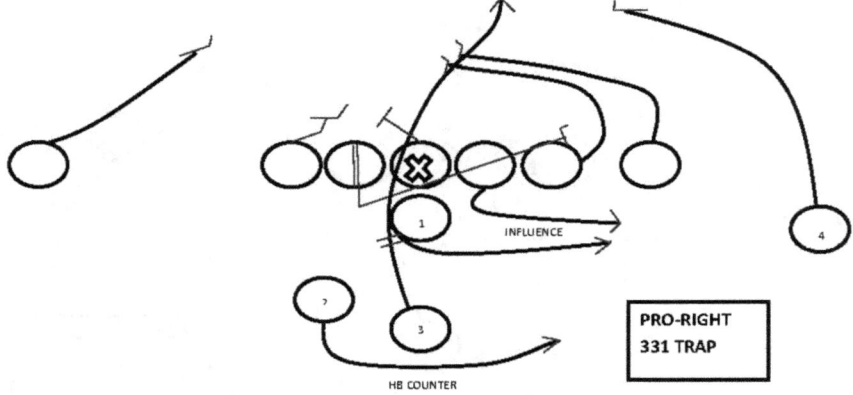

PRO-RIGHT
331 TRAP

INFLUENCE

HB COUNTER

Coach's Note:

1. Fullback Trap

## Sweep Series

**SWEEP SERIES**

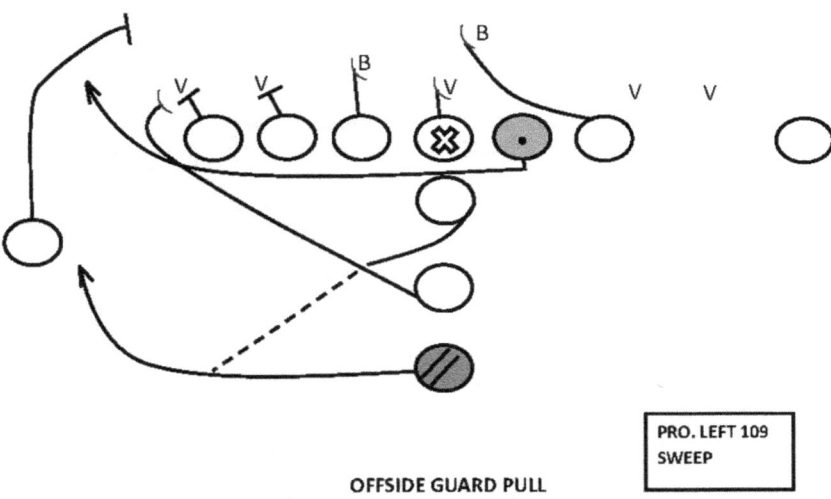

**OFFSIDE GUARD PULL**

PRO. LEFT 109
SWEEP

Coach's Note:

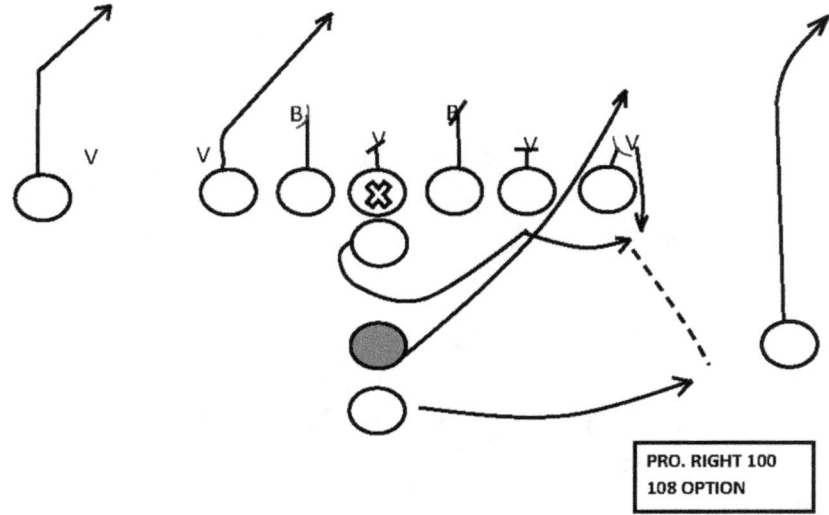

PRO. RIGHT 100
108 OPTION

Offside Guard Pull

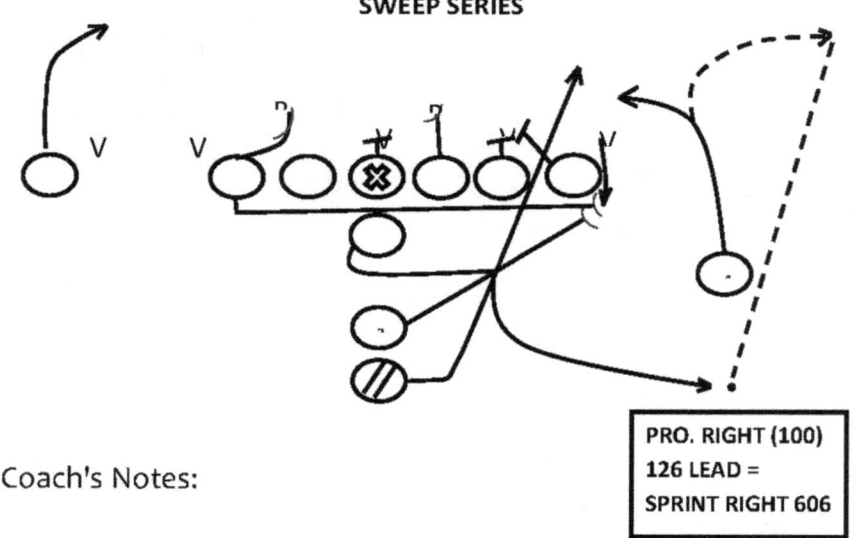

**SWEEP SERIES**

PRO. RIGHT (100)
126 LEAD =
SPRINT RIGHT 606

Coach's Notes:

# SWEEP SERIES

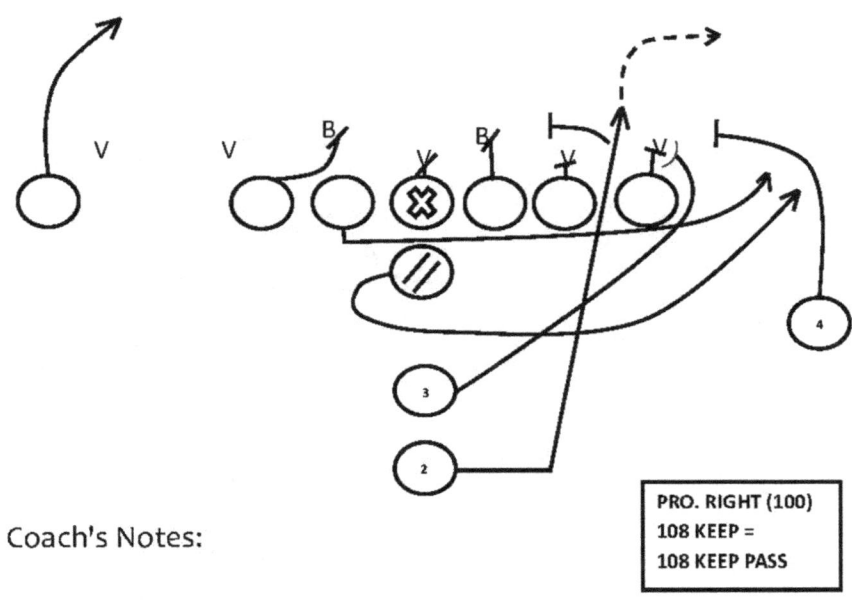

Coach's Notes:

**PRO. RIGHT (100)**
**108 KEEP =**
**108 KEEP PASS**

SWEEP SERIES

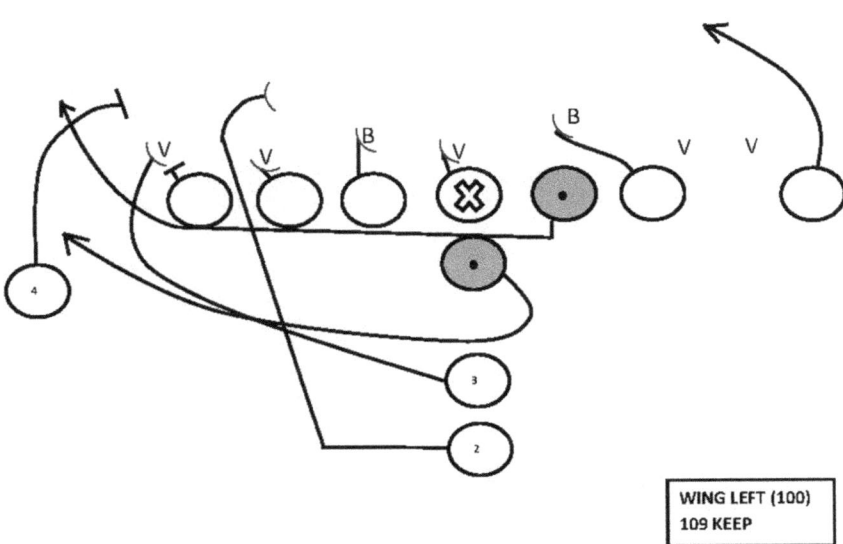

**WING LEFT (100)**
**109 KEEP**

# COUNTER SERIES

**COUNTER**

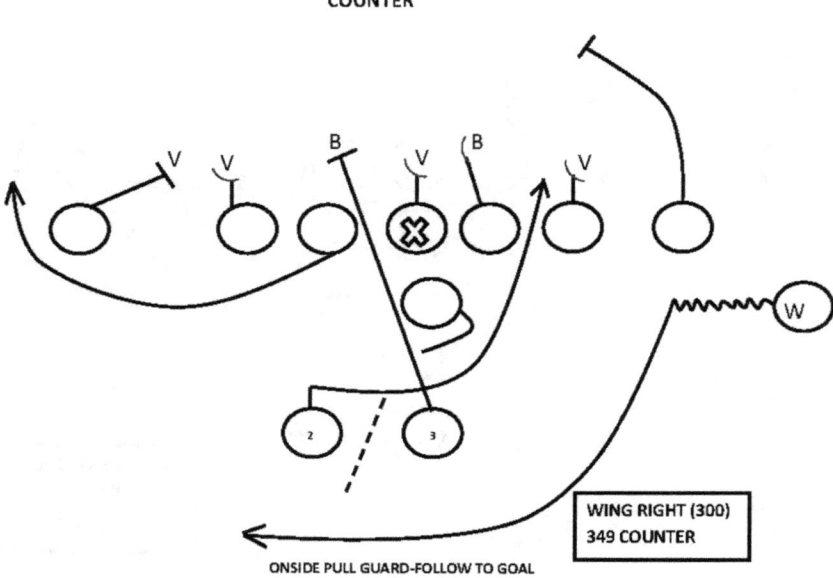

WING RIGHT (300)
349 COUNTER

ONSIDE PULL GUARD-FOLLOW TO GOAL

Coach's Note:

# COUNTER SEREIS

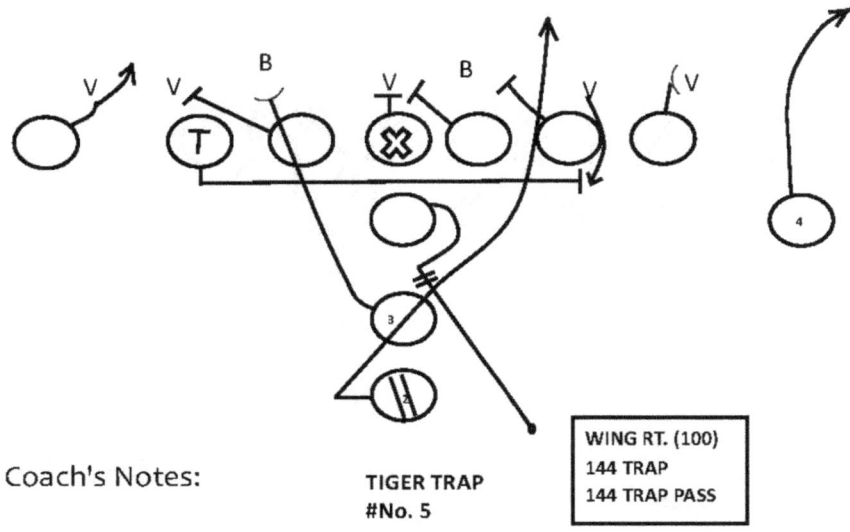

**Coach's Notes:**

**TIGER TRAP**
**#No. 5**

WING RT. (100)
144 TRAP
144 TRAP PASS

## COUNTER SERIES

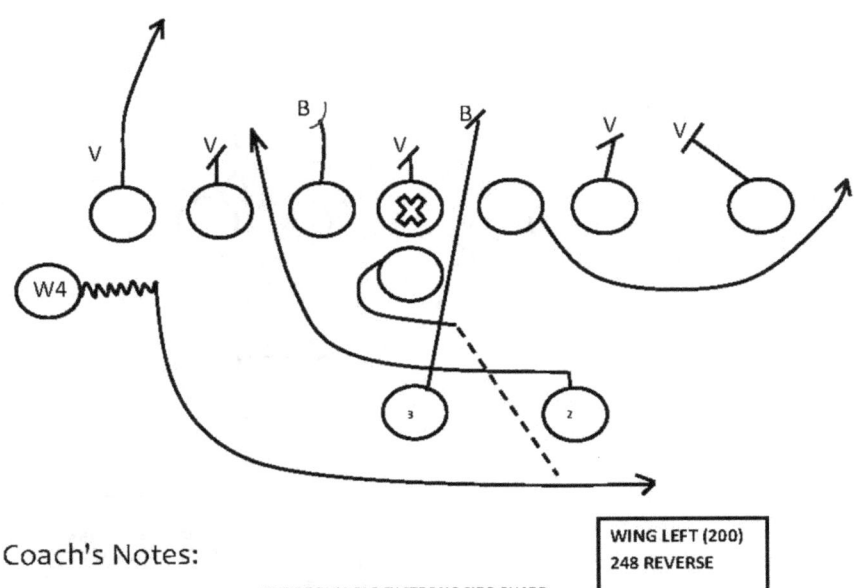

**Coach's Notes:**

ONSIDE PULL BLOCK STRONG SIDE GUARD

WING LEFT (200)
248 REVERSE

# COUNTER SERIES

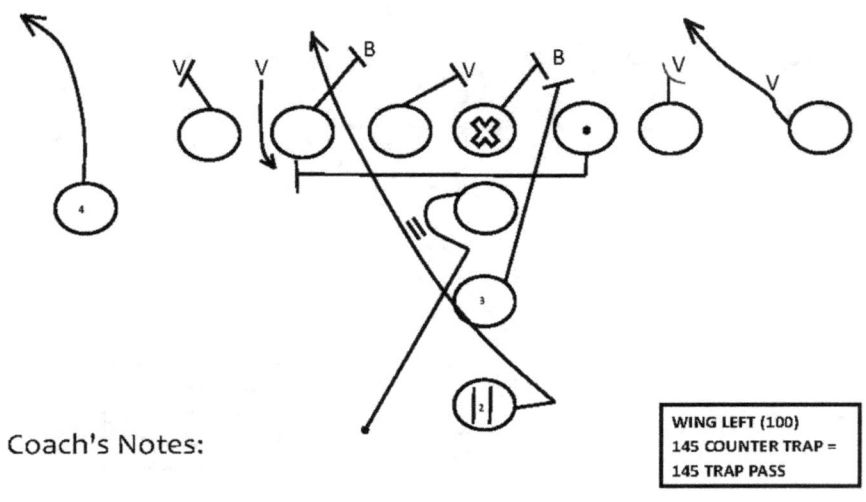

**Coach's Notes:**

**WING LEFT (100)**
**145 COUNTER TRAP =**
**145 TRAP PASS**

**COUNTER SERIES**

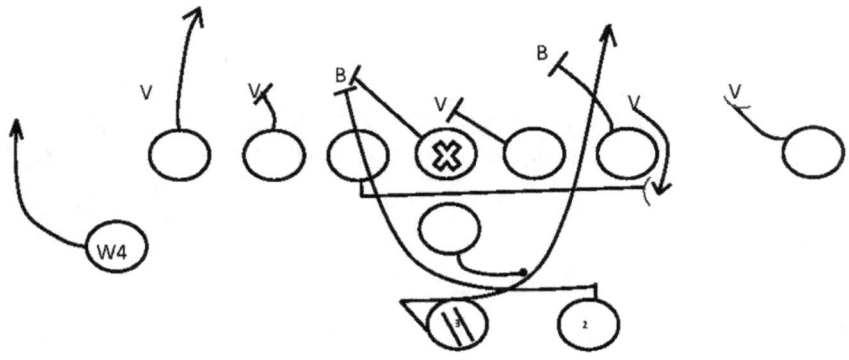

**Coach's Notes:**

TRAP BLOCK ON #5 TECHNIQUE

**WING LEFT (200)**
**244 COUNTER TRAP**

# COUNTER SERIES

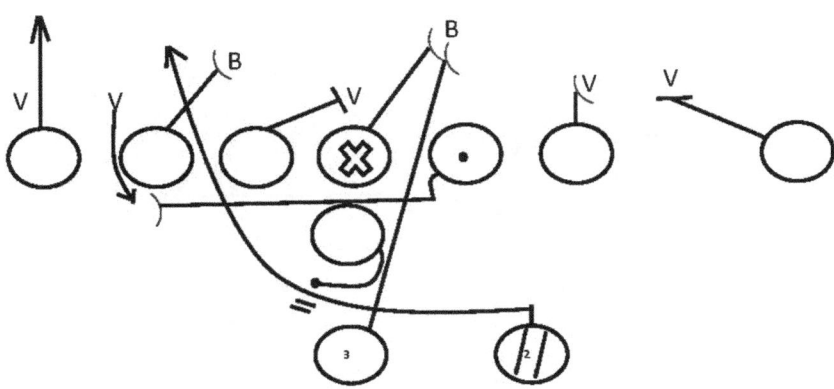

**Coach's Notes:**

TRAP BLOCK ON #5 TECHNIQUE

TRAP/COUNTER SERIES

> SLOT RT. (200)
> 243 COUNTER TRAP

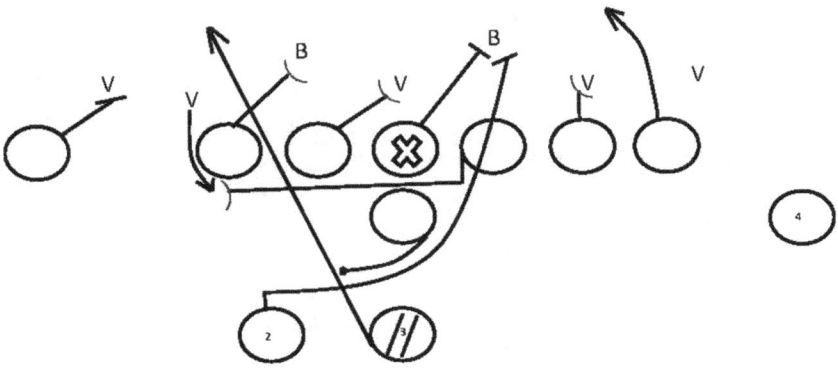

> WING RIGHT (300)
> 343 COUNTER TRAP

**Coach's Notes:**

# TRAP/COUNTER SERIES

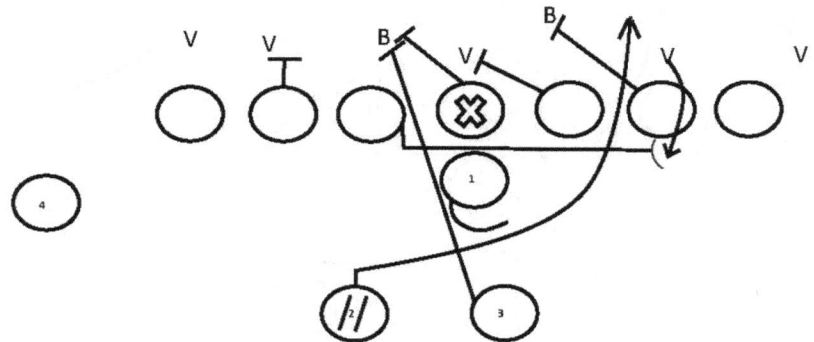

**WING LEFT (300)**
**344 COUNTER TRAP**

**DOUBLE TEAM STRONG LB OR SAFETY**

**COUNTER OPTION TO TIGHT END**

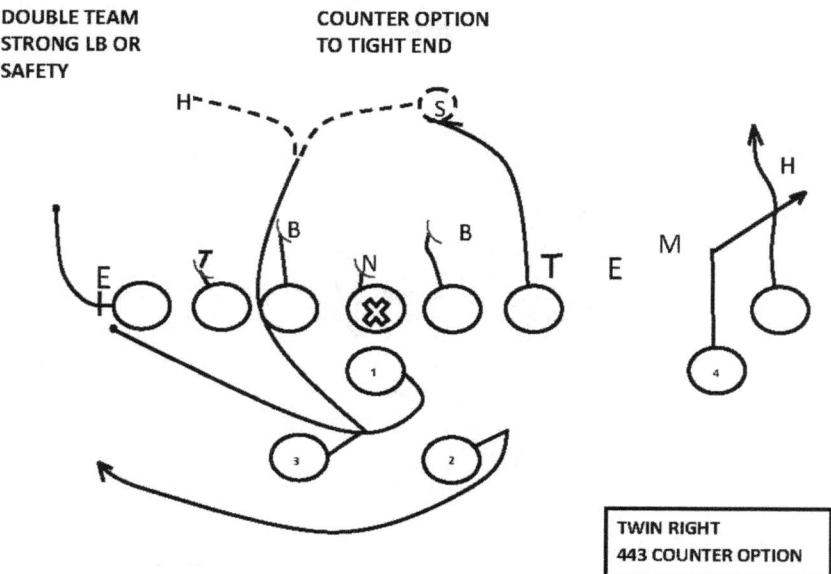

**TWIN RIGHT**
**443 COUNTER OPTION**

Coach's Notes:

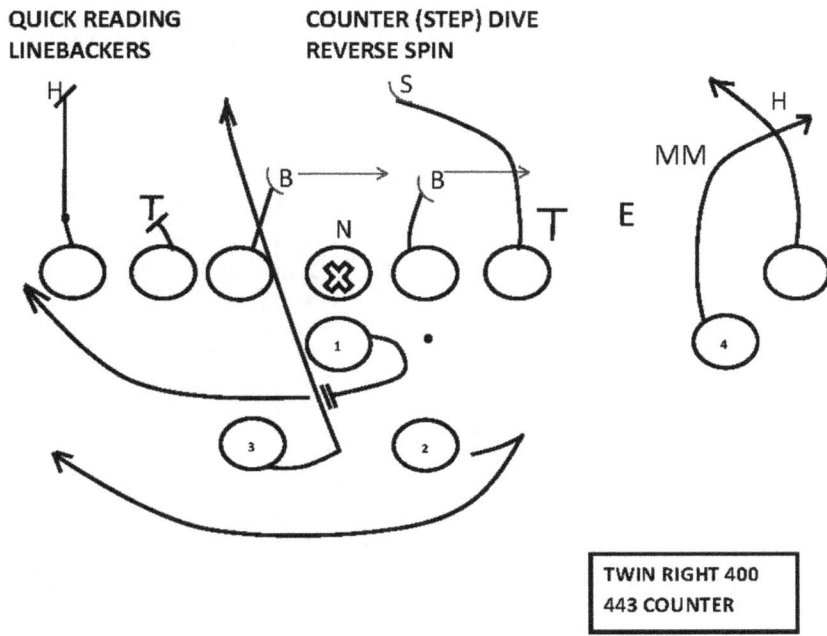

## QUICK READING LINEBACKERS

## COUNTER (STEP) DIVE REVERSE SPIN

TWIN RIGHT 400
443 COUNTER

## 3-M AN PASS (2-MAN UNDER)

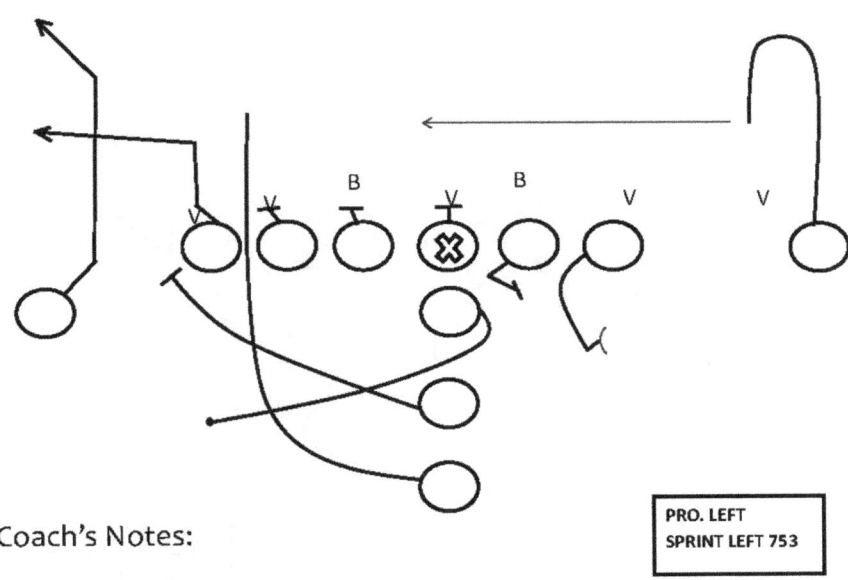

PRO. LEFT
SPRINT LEFT 753

Coach's Notes:

## 3-M AN PASS (2-BACK UNDER)

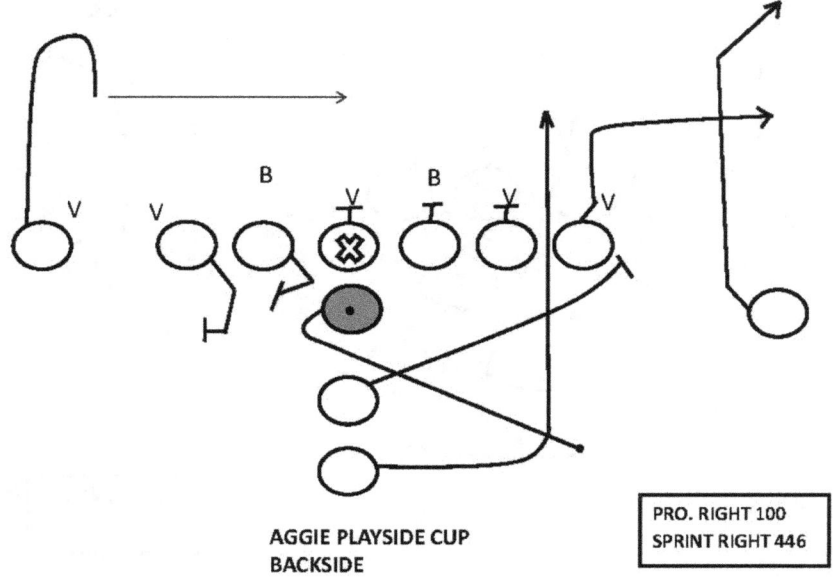

**AGGIE PLAYSIDE CUP
BACKSIDE**

PRO. RIGHT 100
SPRINT RIGHT 446

## 3-MAN PASS (2-BACK OUT)

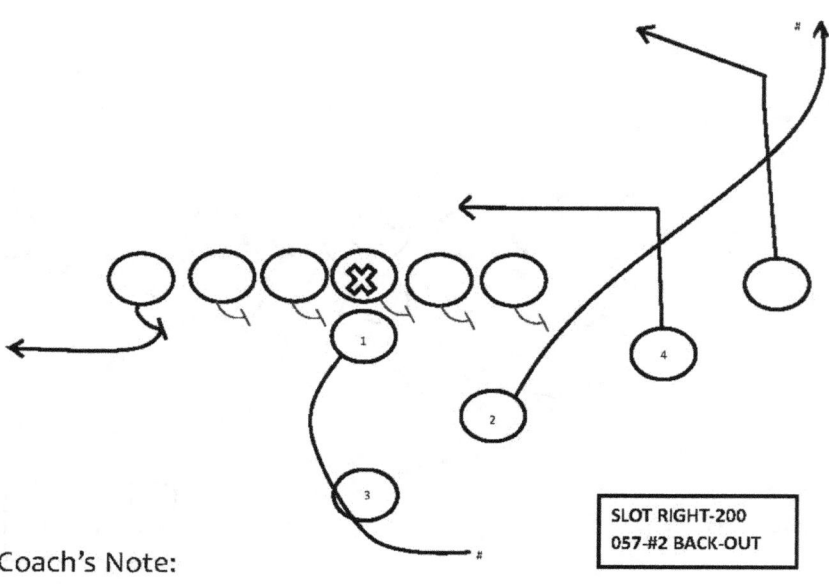

SLOT RIGHT-200
057-#2 BACK-OUT

Coach's Note:

# 3- MAN PASS (2-BACK OUT)

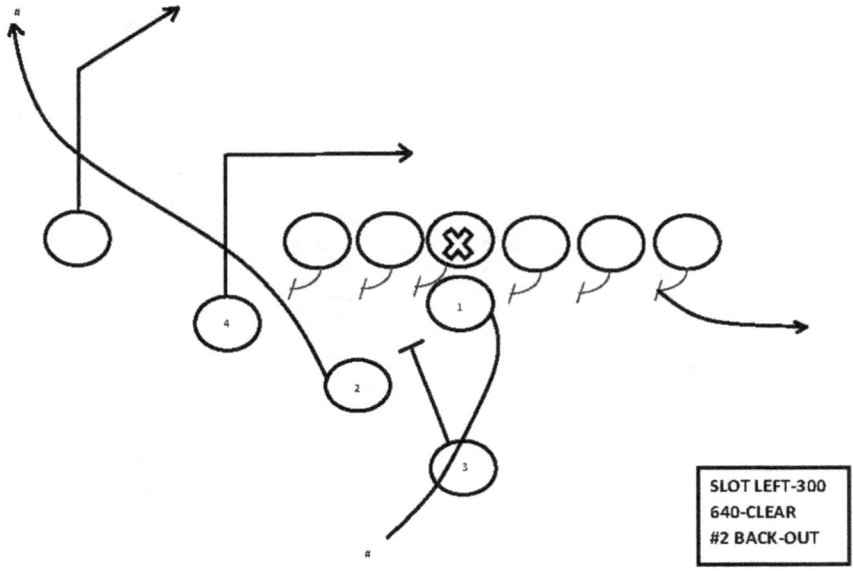

SLOT LEFT-300
640-CLEAR
#2 BACK-OUT

Coach's Notes:

# OPTION – RUN or PASS

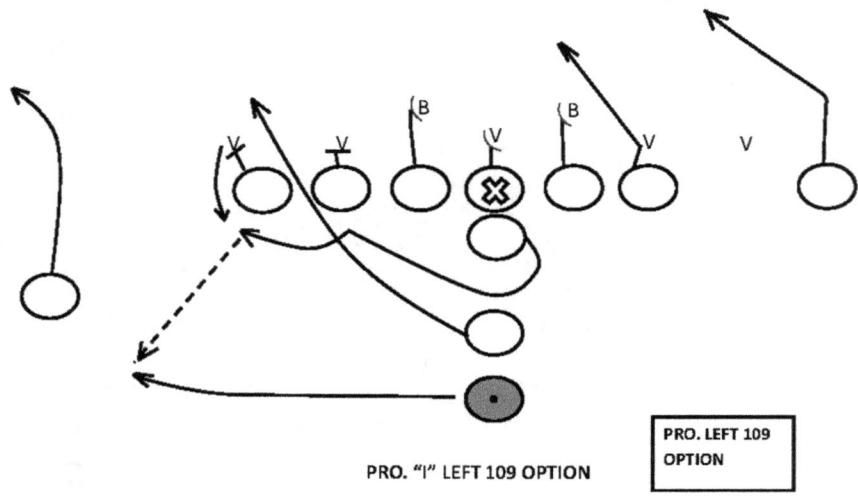

PRO. "I" LEFT 109 OPTION

PRO. LEFT 109 OPTION

Coach's Note:

1. 209 Option

2. 109 Option

# OPTION – RUN or PASS

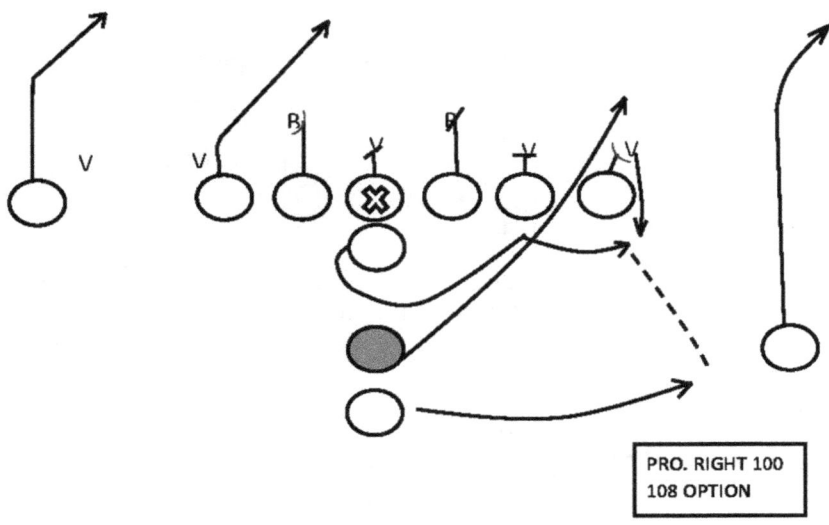

PRO. RIGHT 100
108 OPTION

Coach's Note:

1. 308 Option

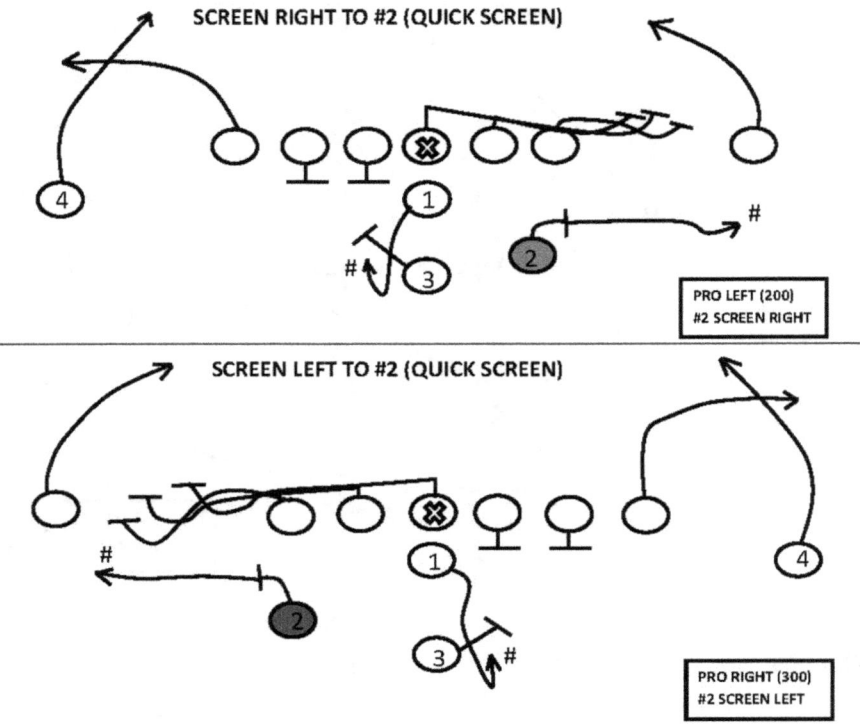

Coach's Note:

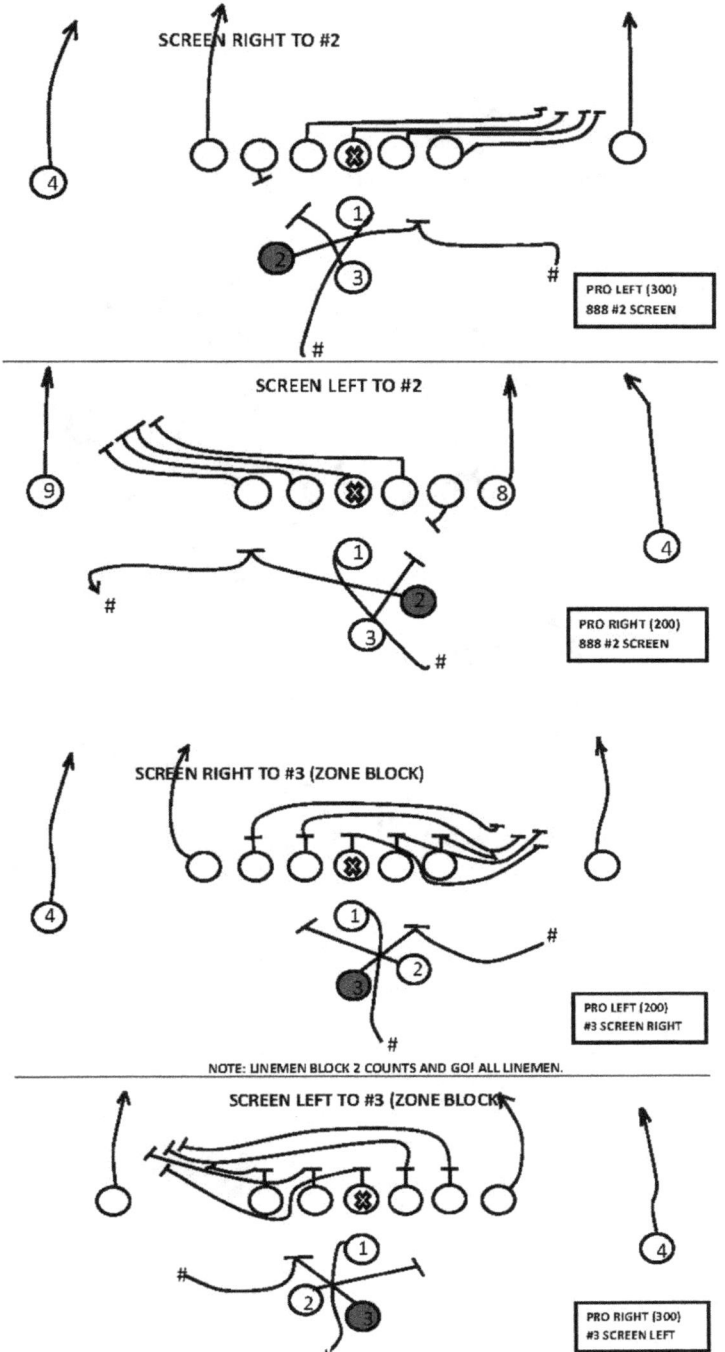

SCREEN RIGHT TO #2

PRO LEFT (300)
888 #2 SCREEN

SCREEN LEFT TO #2

PRO RIGHT (200)
888 #2 SCREEN

SCREEN RIGHT TO #3 (ZONE BLOCK)

PRO LEFT (200)
#3 SCREEN RIGHT

NOTE: LINEMEN BLOCK 2 COUNTS AND GO! ALL LINEMEN.

SCREEN LEFT TO #3 (ZONE BLOCK)

PRO RIGHT (300)
#3 SCREEN LEFT

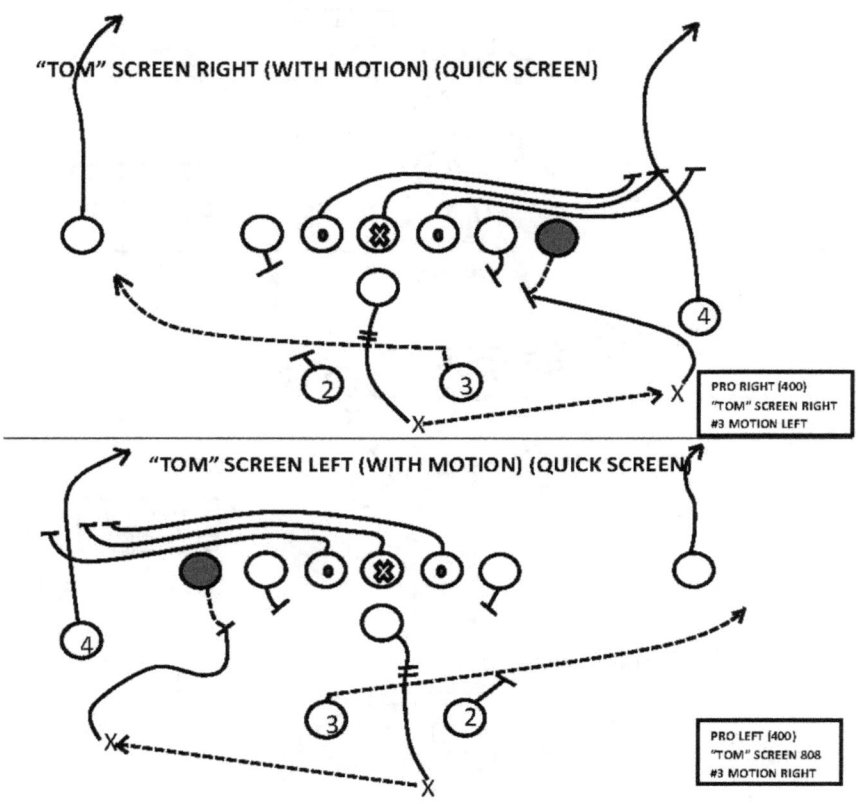

**"TOM" SCREEN RIGHT (WITH MOTION) (QUICK SCREEN)**

PRO RIGHT (400)
"TOM" SCREEN RIGHT
#3 MOTION LEFT

**"TOM" SCREEN LEFT (WITH MOTION) (QUICK SCREEN)**

PRO LEFT (400)
"TOM" SCREEN 808
#3 MOTION RIGHT

Coach's Note:

## 3-MAN PASS

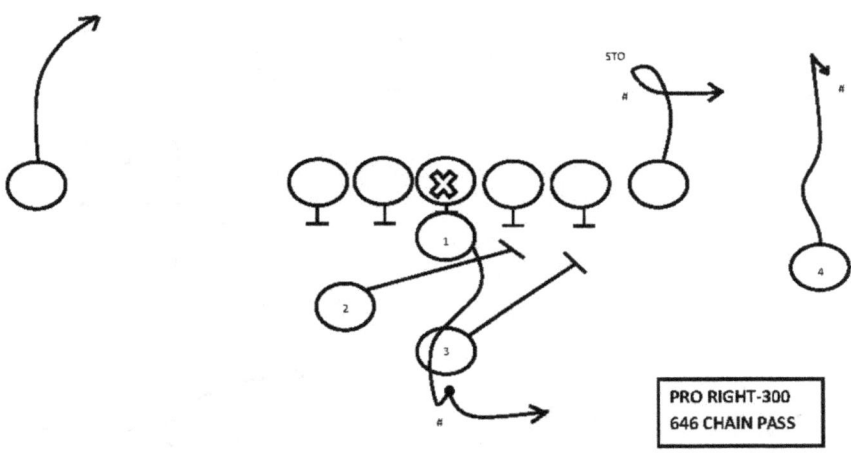

PRO RIGHT-300
646 CHAIN PASS

Coach's Notes:

## 3-MAN PASS

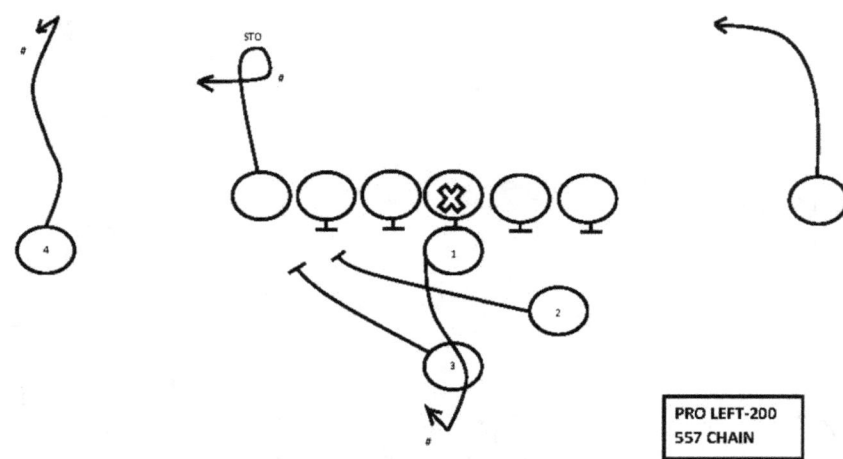

PRO LEFT-200
557 CHAIN

## 3-MAN PATTERN

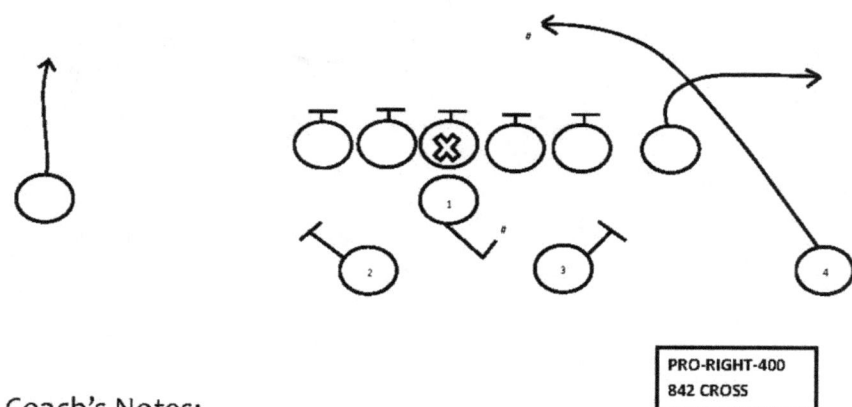

PRO-RIGHT-400
842 CROSS

Coach's Notes:

## 3-MAN PATTERN

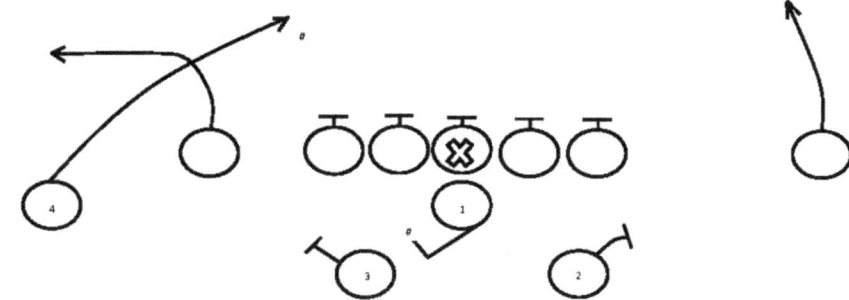

## 3-MAN PASS

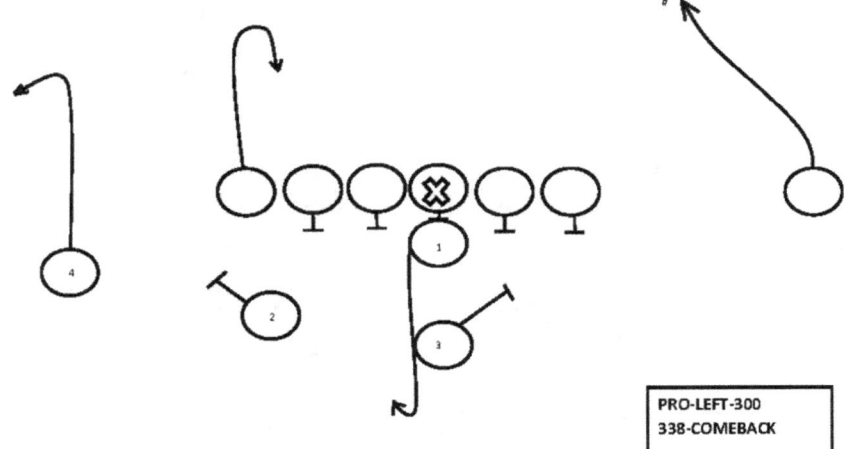

PRO-LEFT-300
338-COMEBACK

Coach's Notes:

## 3-MAN PATTERN

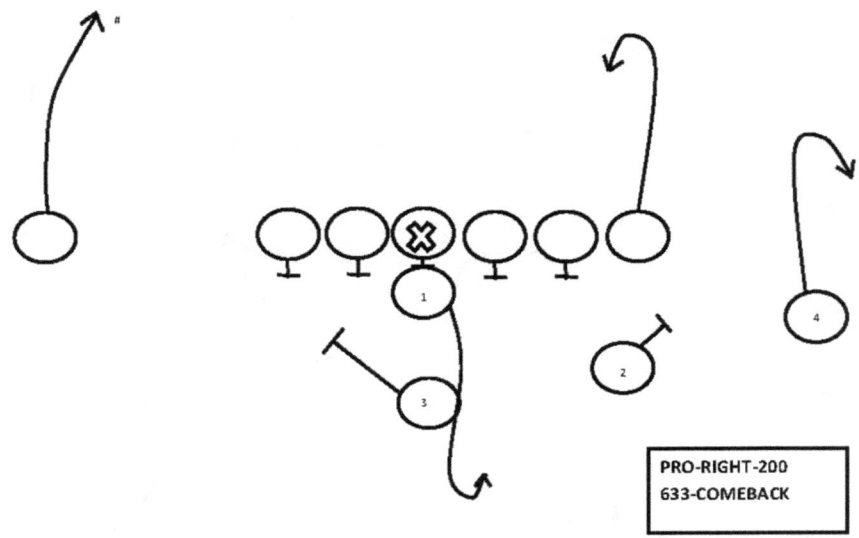

PRO-RIGHT-200
633-COMEBACK

## 3-MAN PATTERN

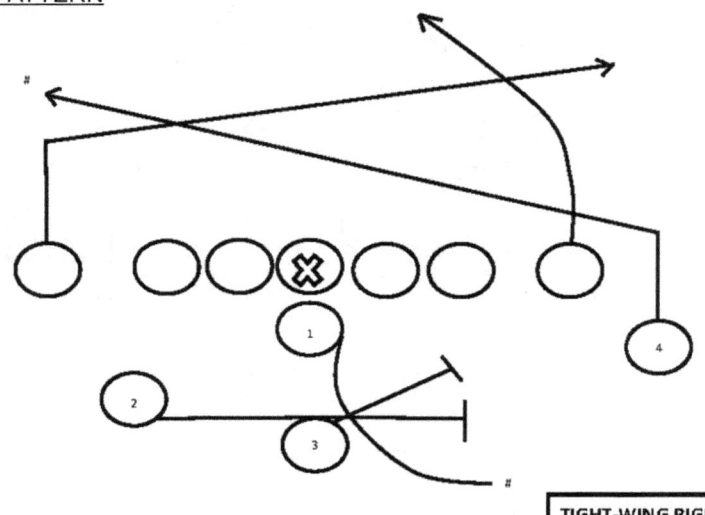

TIGHT-WING RIGHT
SPRINT RIGHT
457-#4 DELAY

Coach's Notes:

3-MAN

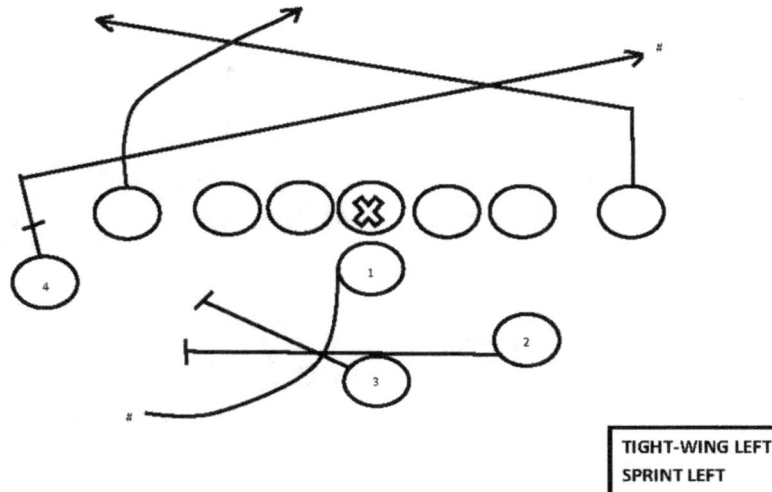

**TIGHT-WING LEFT**
**SPRINT LEFT**
**467-#4 DELAY**

3-MAN PATTERN
(Short Side of Field)

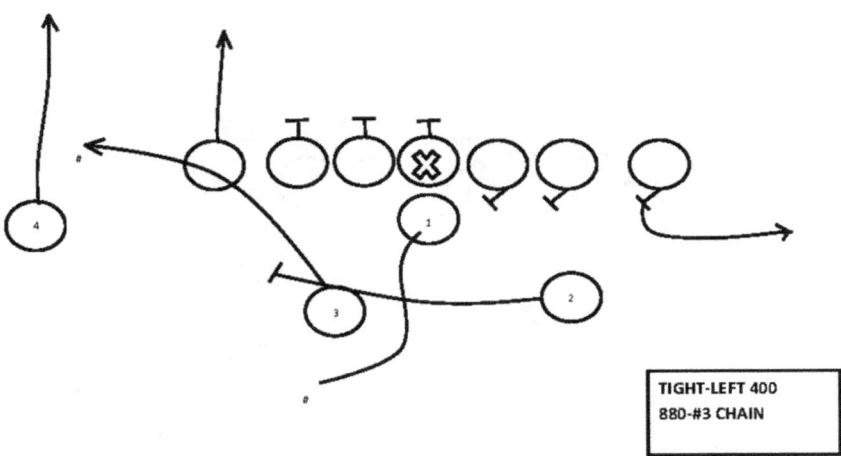

**TIGHT-LEFT 400**
**880-#3 CHAIN**

## 3-MAN PATTERN

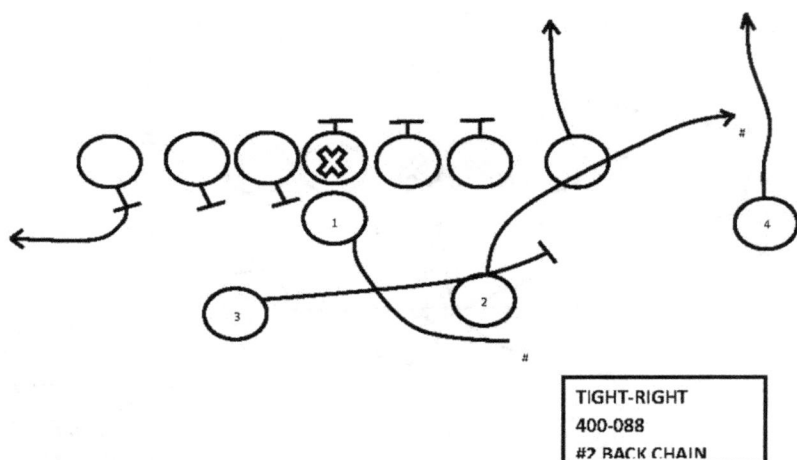

TIGHT-RIGHT
400-088
#2 BACK CHAIN

## 3-MAN

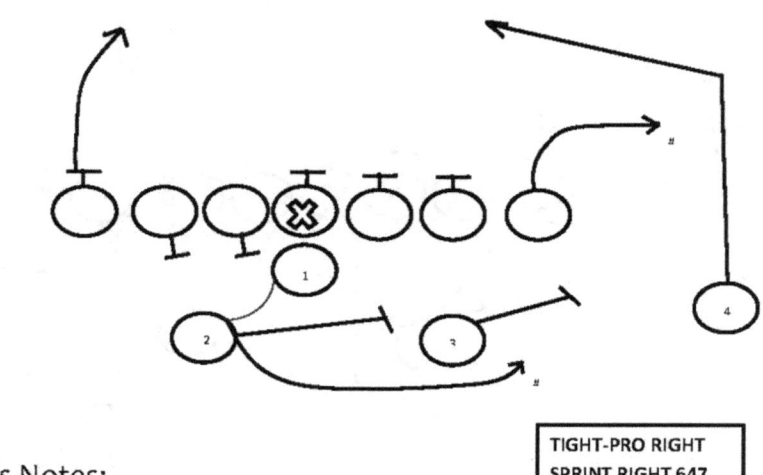

Coach's Notes:

TIGHT-PRO RIGHT
SPRINT RIGHT 647

## 3-MAN PASS

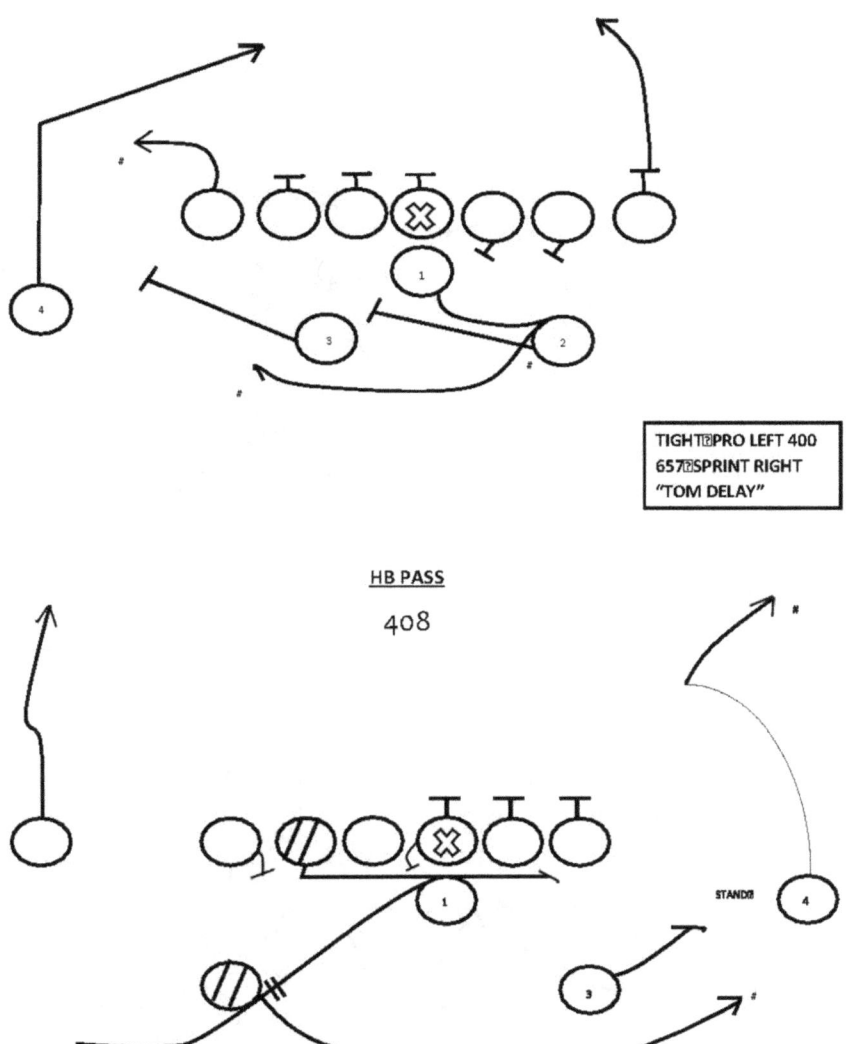

TIGHT⬚PRO LEFT 400
657⬚SPRINT RIGHT
"TOM DELAY"

## HB PASS

408

Coach's Notes:

## HB PASS

### 409

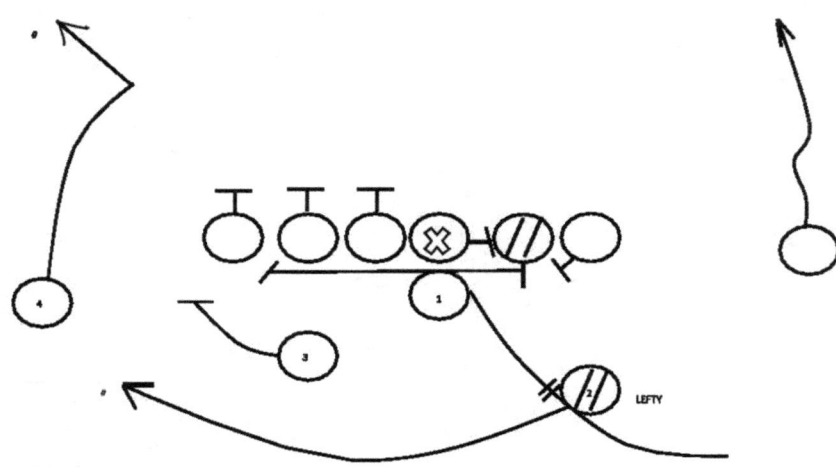

## 3 MAN (Clear 777)

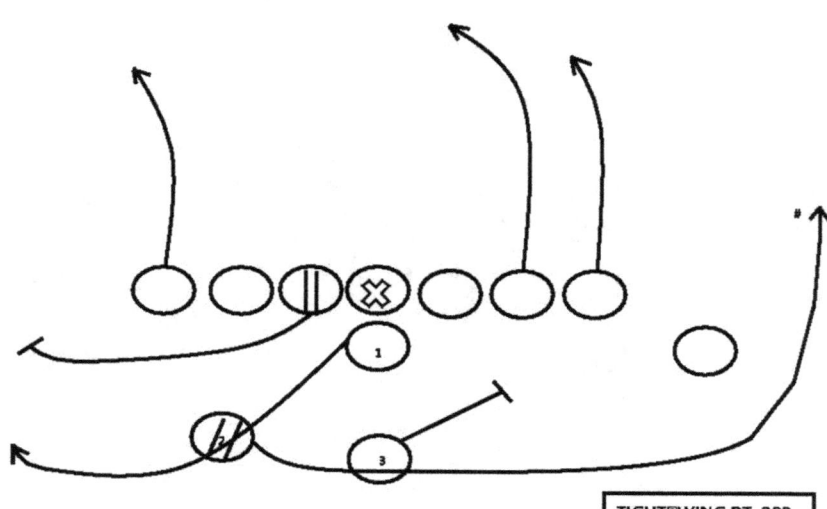

TIGHT▢WING RT. 300
SPRINT LEFT 777
#2 THROW BACK

Coach's Notes:

## QB THROW BACK

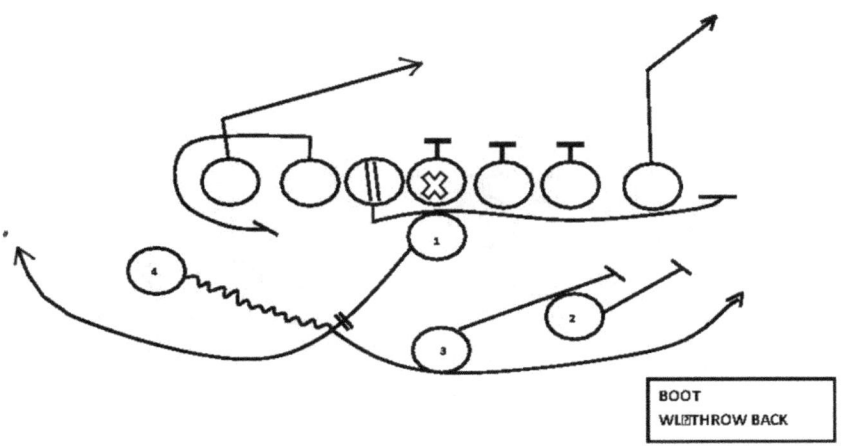

BOOT
WL THROW BACK

## QB THROW FAKE

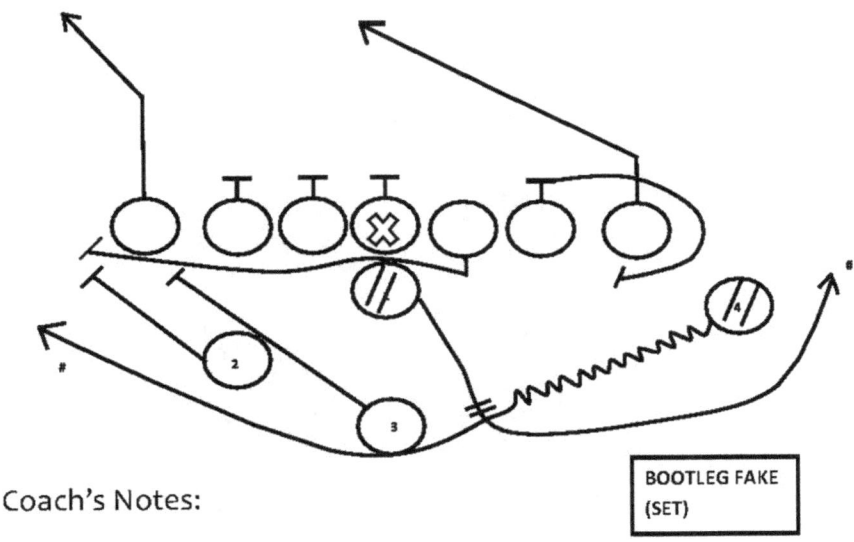

BOOTLEG FAKE
(SET)

Coach's Notes:

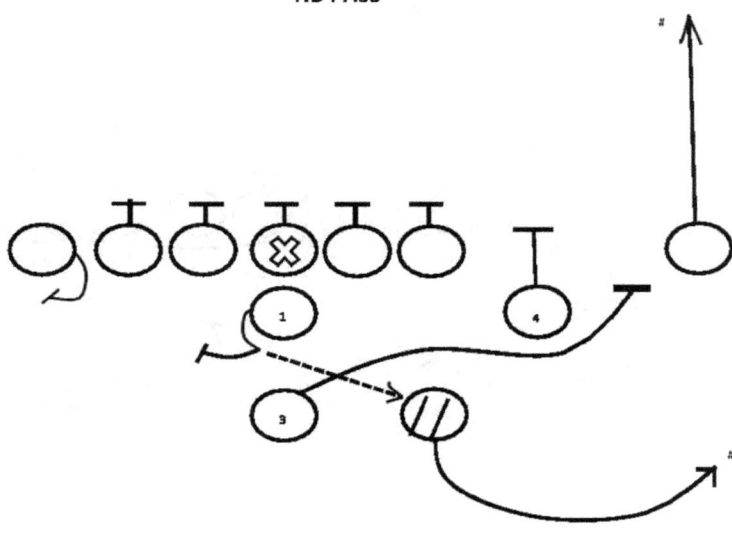

**SUCKER SERIES**
**HB PASS**

Slot Right 208
HB-Pass

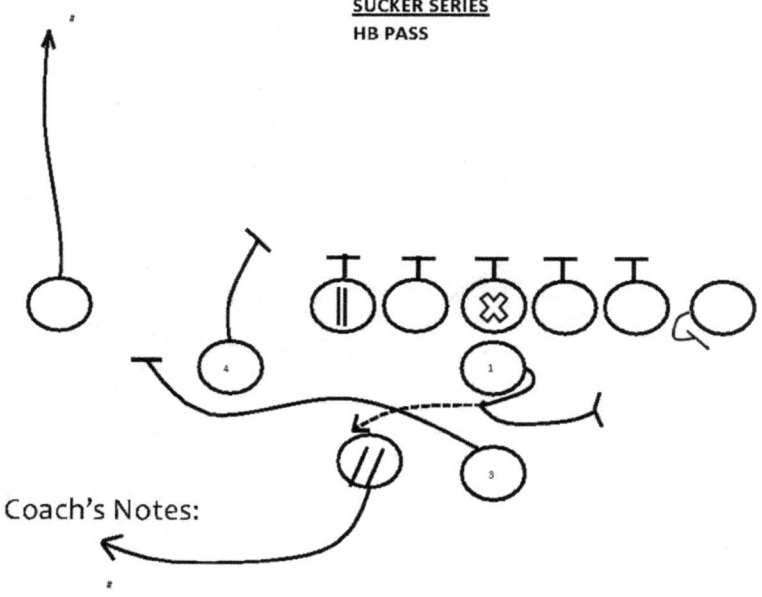

**SUCKER SERIES**
**HB PASS**

Coach's Notes:

**DRAW SERIES**

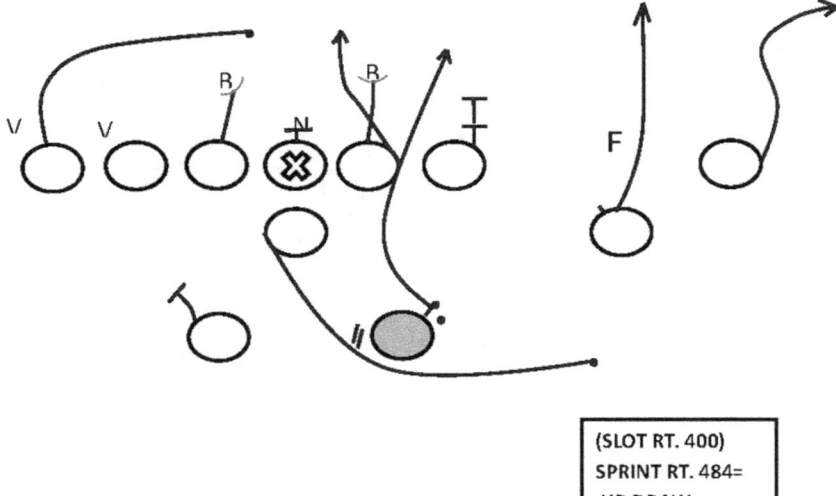

(SLOT RT. 400)
SPRINT RT. 484=
  HB DRAW

Coach's Notes:

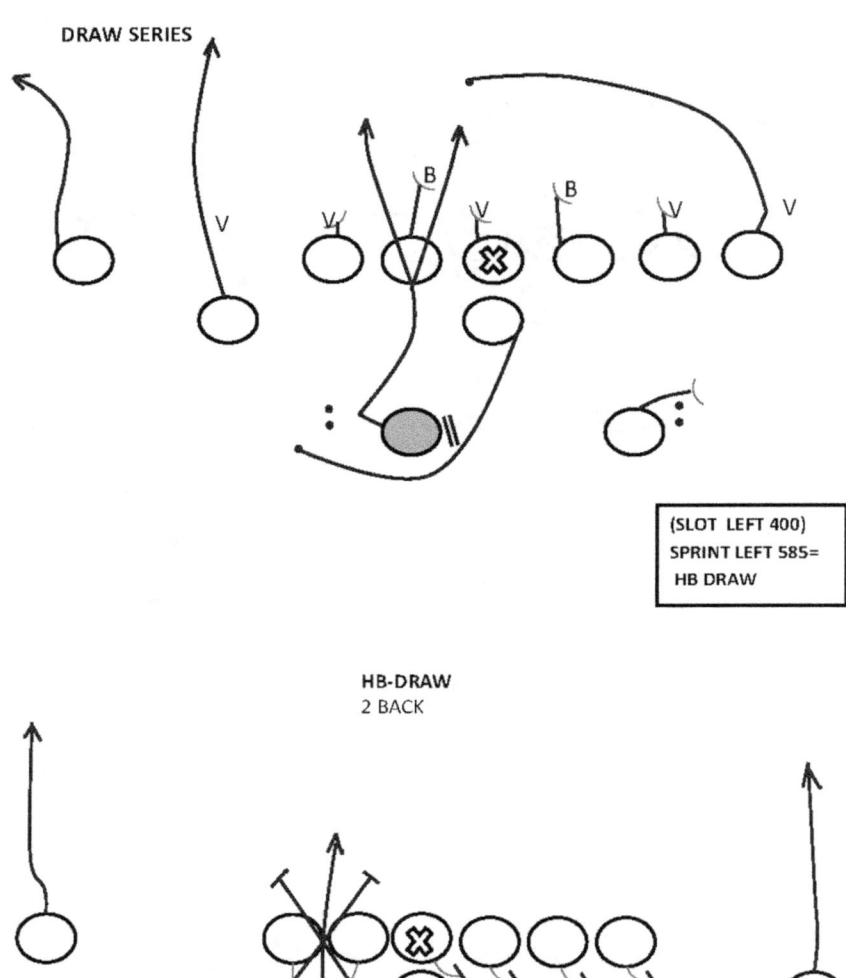

**DRAW SERIES**

(SLOT LEFT 400)
SPRINT LEFT 585=
HB DRAW

**HB-DRAW**
2 BACK

PRO RIGHT
233 BELLY
HB DRAW 233 BELLY

Coach's Notes:

**HB-DRAW**
BACK

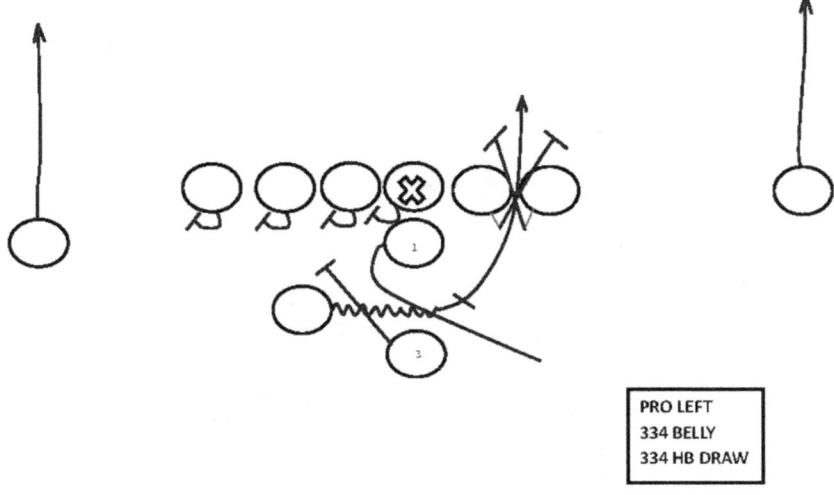

PRO LEFT
334 BELLY
334 HB DRAW

**STATUE OF LIBERTY**

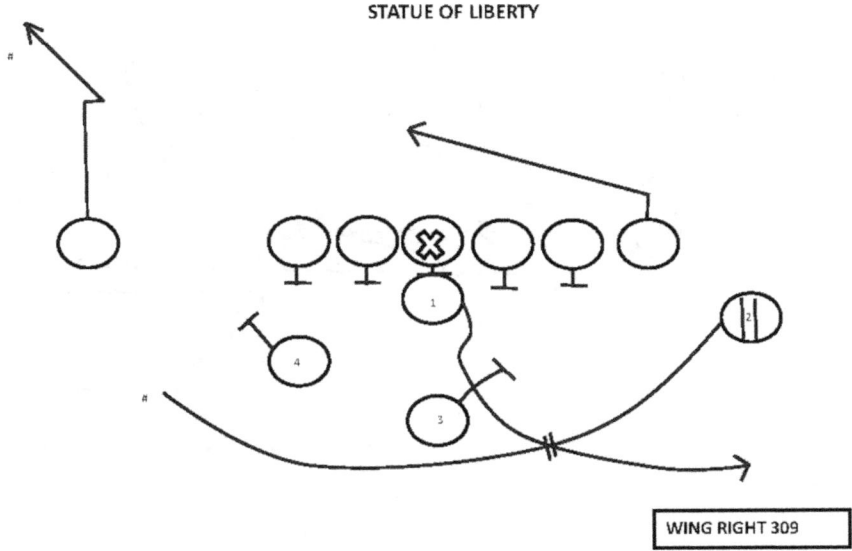

WING RIGHT 309

Coach's Notes:

# STATUE OF LIBERTY

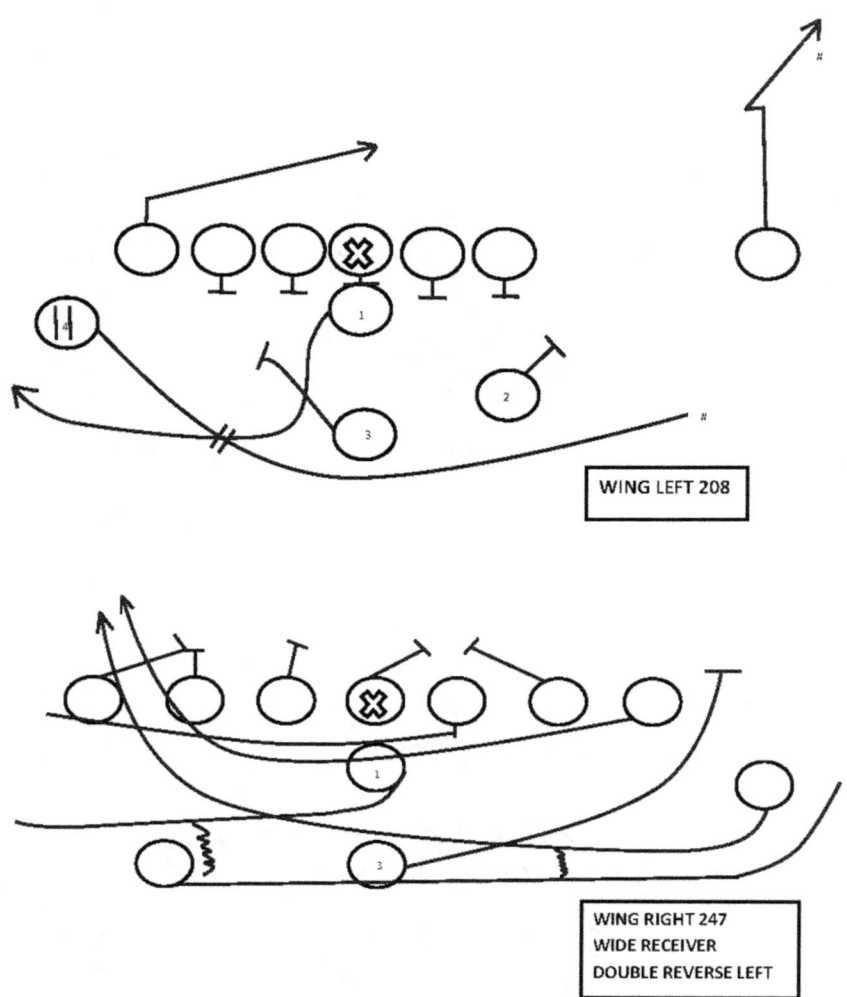

WING LEFT 208

WING RIGHT 247
WIDE RECEIVER
DOUBLE REVERSE LEFT

Coach's Note:

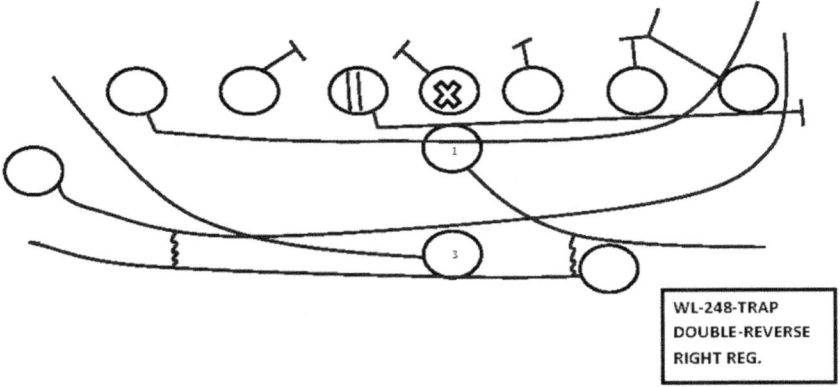

WL-248-TRAP
DOUBLE-REVERSE
RIGHT REG.

Coach's Note:

www.ingramcontent.com/pod-product-compliance
Lightning Source LLC
Chambersburg PA
CBHW061701120626
46550CB00003B/1038